Numerology
for
Decoding
Behavior

Numerology *for* Decoding Behavior

Your Personal Numbers at Work, with Family, and in Relationships

MICHAEL BRILL

Destiny Books
Rochester, Vermont • Toronto, Canada

Destiny Books
One Park Street
Rochester, Vermont 05767
www.DestinyBooks.com

SUSTAINABLE FORESTRY INITIATIVE   Certified Sourcing
www.sfiprogram.org
SFI-00854

Text stock is SFI certified

Destiny Books is a division of Inner Traditions International

Library of Congress Cataloging-in-Publication Data

Brill, Michael (Michael Richard)
  Numerology for decoding behavior : your personal numbers at work, with family,
and in relationships / Michael Brill.
     p. cm.
  Includes index.
  ISBN 978-1-59477-374-7 (pbk.) — ISBN 978-1-59477-941-1 (ebook)
  1. Numerology. 2. Interpersonal relations—Miscellanea. I. Title.
  BF1623.P9B659 2011
  133.3'35—dc22

                                                                    2011015063

Printed and bound in the United States by Lake Book Manufacturing
The text stock is SFI certified. The Sustainable Forestry Initiative® program pro-
motes sustainable forest management.

10 9 8 7 6 5 4 3 2 1

Text design and layout by Priscilla Baker
This book was typeset in Garamond Premier Pro with Perpetua and Gill Sans
used as display typefaces

To send correspondence to the author of this book, mail a first-class letter to the
author c/o Inner Traditions • Bear & Company, One Park Street, Rochester, VT
05767, and we will forward the communication or contact the author directly at
www.awakener.com.

Dedicated with love to
Boonchalong Mulakul.
After a thousand years, we have
found each other again.
Let's make it happen.

Contents

Introduction

Every *thing* in our universe vibrates at a specific frequency that can be identified and mathematically measured. Whatever exists can be symbolically represented by a number; numbers are thus the visible manifestation of the building blocks of creation. The system I have developed, known as Cosmic Numerology, reveals behavioral insights derived from the mathematical patterns associated with the numbers and letters that make up our realities. The letters of any name can be used to determine emotional and psychological characteristics and behavior patterns for a business or an individual. The birth data of an individual or business identifies their potential for making either reactive or proactive choices.

Cosmic Numerology can deconstruct these patterns, with the use of what I refer to as "quantum numbers," which make it possible for us to understand, measure, and interpret combinations of patterns as they manifest themselves in our realities.

The purpose of this book is to assist you to better understand some of the underlying causes of reactive behavior patterns, whether in yourself or others. What you will find here are simple mathematical formulas that will enable you to quickly identify your own or another person's core issues and strengths, while gaining a better understanding of why individuals behave the way they do at work, in their relationships, and with their families. There is a technique for identifying core issues and their "soulutions" (solutions chosen by the soul) and a method that will enable you to decipher behavior patterns associated with the first vowel/consonant combinations of names.

The simple formulas discussed in this book provide quick and accurate ways of gaining insights into the mental and emotional motives of children, family members, partners, clients, customers, and employees. Understanding and using this knowledge will lead to more successful interactions with others, which in turn will bring more abundance.

These techniques can be used in business to gain an advantage over the competition by better understanding each client's or competitor's needs and behavior patterns. Those in sales will be able to identify a client's behavior patterns and tailor their presentation to increase the probability of a sale.

Human resource departments can incorporate this information and use it to assist participants in their employee assistance programs. These formulas can be applied to building balanced teams within an organization, to facilitating better employee communication and interaction, for conflict resolution, even for assisting employees to find their "happy spot" within the organization.

Mental health professionals can use this information to shorten the time it takes to identify someone's underlying motivations. Social workers, especially those working with children and adolescents, can zero in on some of their clients' core issues within minutes.

Health practitioners can get a thumbnail sketch of a client's emotional and psychological behavior patterns. These behaviors are also part of an overall pattern that is the catalyst for specific health issues (e.g., illnesses, diseases, and injuries.)

Educators can quickly identify the behavioral as well as the learning patterns of individual students, thus enabling them to personalize instruction.

Parents and grandparents can help maximize their children's strengths by helping them make more proactive decisions and fewer reactive decisions.

Individuals seeking personal insights will also find the information in this book to be useful.

This book is simple to use. It will lead you step by step through the methods of Cosmic Numerology, with clear instructions for their application.

- Chapter 1 provides an introduction to Cosmic Numerology. It also describes the origins of two universal behavior patterns, control and codependency, and indicates how quantum numbers can be used to identify these patterns as a first step to transforming them. It presents the basic number concepts and an interpretation of the positive and negative characteristics of the numbers 1 through 9.

- Chapter 2 describes how to identify any person's core issues (via their achievement number) using just their month and day of birth. *Core issues* are the behaviors that influence all areas of a life. The achievement number determines both reactive and proactive behavior choices.

- Chapter 3 presents the map I have developed of the basic patterns of the human personality matrix and makes it clear how you can use it to find the soulution to any achievement number challenge.

- Chapter 4 introduces two formulas you can use to identify specific behavior patterns at work, in relationships, and with family, both based on the letter-to-number conversion of names. The first is the formula for using the 1st Vowel/Consonant Challenge (V/CC); the second is the sum of the numbers corresponding to all the letters in a name.

- Chapter 5 puts another layer of interpretation at your disposal through the use of the *Table of Personality Characteristics,* based on the distribution of the letters of the alphabet through the four planes of expression: mental, physical, emotional, and intuitive. This is an invaluable tool of behavioral interpretation that can be applied in any life context.

- Chapter 6 provides specific examples targeting the application of these methods and insights in business, sales, management, marketing, mental health, social work, education, and parenting.

- Appendix I supplements chapter 4 with a complete *Table of Predefined 1st Vowel/1st Consonant Challenges (V/CC)*, in which you can look up the interpretation of any number combination derived from the V/CC of any name.

- Appendix II has practice worksheets for your use as you apply the methods of Cosmic Numerology at home and at work, for a more fulfilling and abundant life.

I believe that we have all consciously chosen the letters for our names, our birth date, and our birth or adoptive family, and we have all made certain we have a written guarantee for success. The written guarantee includes built-in soulutions (conscious proactive choices) for resolving every life challenge. As long as we pursue abundance, thinking it will bring safety and security, it will elude us, because we will never feel secure enough. But we can all enter into the flow of abundance through the formulas and knowledge presented in this book. By using these techniques, you will be able to better understand your behavior patterns as well as those of others and to make a conscious choice to live the *soulutions* rather than the challenges.

1

Cosmic Numerology and Quantum Numbers

Cosmic Numerology is the study of the patterns associated with the numbers and letters that make up our potential realities. To identify, classify, or categorize realities, we encode them, using letters, numbers, and symbols. Interpreting these codes, using my version of quantum numbers, can reveal cause-and-effect relationships and the psychological and emotional patterns of individuals, groups, businesses, governments, or countries. Cosmic Numerology melds the sciences of classical numerology and quantum physics with the concepts of the ancient kabbalistic art of gematria and reincarnation.

Numerology—the study of the patterns associated with the numbers and letters that make up our world—is a science because it uses specific formulas with standardized, reproducible results. The numerology formulas used in this book have been derived from the science of numerology developed by Pythagoras, a Greek born in 590 BCE. In classical numerology, the letters of a name and the birth numbers represent the patterns and timing of events to be experienced. In Cosmic Numerology, a force/energy selects the direction of its evolution. In human beings, the letters of the name and the birthday numbers represent a person's life options.

In classical physics there are absolutes, cause and effect, and duality. In quantum physics there are no absolutes; there are potentials and probabilities. Cosmic Numerology sees all energy as frequencies composed of combinations of subfrequencies generated by the blending of the numbers 1 through 9. These combinations are composed of particles (and waves) that ultimately develop a group awareness, which leads to a group consciousness. This can be a group of cells, specific body systems, a country, a galaxy, even a universe.

Gematria is the art of interpreting the energetic relationship of letters, words, phrases, sentences, and paragraphs that have been converted into strings of numbers.

The concept of reincarnation revolves around the idea that we choose what we want to experience in each life. Experiences not completed within a lifetime will be completed in future lifetimes. The premise of Cosmic Numerology is that, at the end of one life cycle, the soul reviews its most recent experiences and adventures in co-creating (e.g., what it has mastered, become proficient at, avoided, hasn't finished, or has procrastinated starting). The second step involves the soul consciously determining what it wants to experience in its upcoming incarnation.

LIFE'S BLUEPRINT

Each of us is a compilation of GOD (or Gathering of Deities) energies, represented by the combination of the numeric frequencies 1 through 9. In fact, all of creation is composed of combinations derived from the purity of these numbers. The core energy of the GOD energies is also described as Spirit, Source, Cosmos, All That Is, Oneness, Creator, and God. Whatever we call it, this core energy needs to be stepped down to be used. We can use a lightning bolt as an analogy. In its pure state, the electricity locked within the lightning can kill us. However, when we harness this power through transformers that can lower its charge, it becomes useable. It can heat our homes, run our factories, cook our food, or light our cities. Similarly, the GOD energy needs to be modified so that creation can take place. When the nine numbers combine their essences, they form a tenth energy, the energy of 0 (zero). This tenth energy is the energy of creation/potential and is usually recognized by humans as what I call "the little 'g' god energy." For science, this is the source of the big bang.

In between lifetimes we choose to be part of the creative process by melding our potential energies with the energy of the cosmos. We review our lives with the god energy before consciously deciding what we will do in our upcoming life. We look at what we have mastered, avoided, refused to release, screwed up, done to excess, and completed. We then decide on the challenges we still need to work on. One of our final acts prior to entering the earthly realm is to verify that we have more than enough grace to succeed; we do. Prior to entering the transition between the celestial realm and the earthly realm, we create a psychological/emotional blueprint of what we intend to experience when we reach our birth destination. This blueprint is composed of the letters of our name, the numbers of our birthday, and the family we choose to join.

Cosmic Numerology enables you to "read this blueprint," using the letters of your name and the numbers of your birthday, to interpret the emotional and psychological characteristics you chose to experience in this lifetime as well as to identify your life's challenges and their (soul-chosen) soulutions.

- Your birth date represents your destiny. This is not a given; it is something you move toward.
- Your first name represents your physical self, health, finances, professional relationships, and how you behave every day (especially at work).
- Your middle name represents your emotional self: your social-emotional behavior patterns, especially in relationships. It is the key

1	2	3	4	5	6	7	8	9
A	B	C	D	E	F	G	H	I
J	K	L	M	N	O	P	Q	R
S	T	U	V	W	X	Y	Z	

8 Cosmic Numerology and Quantum Numbers

to how you behave emotionally and the type of partners to whom you are attracted. Individuals, or cultures, that have no middle name have chosen to focus on learning how to balance their emotions. When there are multiple middle names, they are "squeezed" together to form one name for purposes of analysis.

- Your last name represents the dynamics within the family you have chosen, birth or adoptive. If you were adopted, your birth family either owed you a debt or you owed them; in either case your birth canceled the debt.
- The vowels in your birth name represent your purpose in life, past life patterns, and the soul's direction.
- The consonants, much like the drive shaft in an automobile, represent the energy that drives the physical, emotional, and mental aspects of your ego self (personality). Many of these energy patterns are hidden from public view.
- The total of the letters in your name (the "expression") represents how others see you (your persona or facade), the type of work you prefer, and how you interact with the world.

THE ORIGIN OF OUR ABANDONMENT ISSUES

In addition to this blueprint, our behavior is governed by abandonment issues that arise from our process of transition between the celestial and earthly realms, which causes us to lose our memory of who we truly are and what we volunteered to co-create. This loss of memory is caused by an electric shock, which is generated by the energetic difference between the celestial realm and the earthly realm. As we pass through the transition field, our celestial self, stunned by the frequency shift, goes into a stupor. This temporary "loss of memory" gives the seeds of our abandonment issues the energy to sprout.

Our earthly self, our ego, thrives in this new energy field and

1	2	3	4	5	6	7	8	9
A	B	C	D	E	F	G	H	I
J	K	L	M	N	O	P	Q	R
S	T	U	V	W	X	Y	Z	

Cosmic Numerology and Quantum Numbers   **9**

evolves rapidly into awareness. (This awareness is very much like that of an infant. The infant is aware that something is moving, but is unable to consciously realize that the moving object is its finger and the finger is connected to its body.) The ego awakens in a panic and asks itself, "Where am I? Where is everybody? Why am I alone? Did I do something wrong? Am I being punished? Why is it dark? Have I been betrayed? Am I not loveable?" We feel we've been abandoned or "kicked out" with no explanation. This is because the process of individuation has begun and our celestial self has not fully reconstituted itself. This is the origin of our sense of abandonment. We feel something is missing.

Before we can remember that we are extending from Spirit, not separating from it, and that we *chose* to do so, we enter the process of being birthed as a human being. Again, we don't remember this was our choice; we only feel the pain of our connection (the umbilical cord) being severed. Again we ask ourselves, "What is going on? Why am I alone? Did I do something wrong? Why am I being forced out?" These questions are not answered, and we become anxious, even fearful, thinking that we are alone and abandoned. We think, "This has happened twice. How many more times will I have to experience this pain!?" As we begin life our fear of abandonment begins to influence our choices. We decide, through the EGO (Easing God Out), to adopt a behavior pattern of self-protection. At one extreme our self-protective behavior patterns can manifest as codependency and at the other extreme as the need for total control of the environment.

Codependency can be divided into three subcategories: *clingers, enablers,* and *doers.* Clingers rationalize that "anything is better than being alone"; regardless of how they are treated, they find it almost impossible to leave a relationship. Enablers will support negative behavior patterns because of their desire to be loved. Doers make themselves indispensable. Their rationale is, "I'll do so much for them, they won't be able to get along without me."

Behavior patterns involving control can be divided into two subgroups. The first group consists of individuals who choose not to become emotionally involved or attached to anything. In essence, they hide or deny their emotions and feelings. They reason that if they don't connect to something, they won't have to experience becoming disconnected from it. The most extreme example is the sociopathic personality. The second subgroup decides that their safest route is to "do for others," but not let anyone "do for them" or "to them." For example, they will hold the handle of a water fountain so that others may drink in ease, but will not let anyone hold the handle for them for fear that the holder will let go. They feel that "others" cannot be depended on. (They may also become agitated about no one offering to "do for them.")

Most of us fit somewhere along the spectrum between these extremes; we have some codependency issues and some control issues. We're like water sloshing back and forth in a tube. Our goal is to recognize our issues through our life challenges. Once we recognize our patterns, we can become proactive rather than reactive. Our souls did not choose to come to earth to experience pain and suffering. They chose to come here as co-creators. However, feelings associated with abandonment block the memories associated with being Divine.

Quantum numbers can identify the underlying patterns of negative behavior that are the result of false cellular memories of feeling abandoned or being punished for some unknown act, which began when we chose to become co-creators and individualize in physical form, and which will end when we remember that even in physical form we are part of the divine energy of creation.

INTERPRETATIONS OF NUMBERS 1–9 AND 0

It is imperative to *know your numbers* because numbers are the basic ingredients of the patterns of creation. All numbers are composed of the single digits 1 through 9. Once a person, place, or thing is identified—whether its origin is mineral, vegetable, or animal; liquid, solid, or gaseous—its alphanumeric identifiers (letters and numbers) can be transposed into a single digit, each with its basic concept. For example, the concept for 1 is "issues of the ego self"; number 2 is "issues involving others." Use of the following table will allow you to quickly interpret the basic meaning of any number.

TABLE OF BASIC NUMBER CONCEPTS

1 = Issues of the Ego Self

2 = Issues Involving Others

3 = Issues Involving Communication, Social Interactions, Feelings of Inadequacy

4 = Issues Involving Details and "Getting Things Done"

5 = Issues Involving Change and Movement

6 = Issues Involving Family, Community, Relationships, Responsibility

7 = Issues Involving Abandonment, Trust, Skepticism, and Control

8 = Issues Involving Power, Money, Control, and Status

9 = Issues Involving Selflessness

0 = Issues Related to Spirit

Once you are proficient with these basic numeric concepts, then you can begin learning the positive and negative characteristics of each number, which will allow you to look at your individual patterns as well as those of others, or of any element of the universe.

Positive and Negative Energy of Numbers

Our universe is composed of energy. This energy has both a positive and negative charge to it. According to science, negative particles of energy are larger than positive particles of energy. You can visualize positive energy as a smooth, round BB and negative energy as being somewhat larger with an irregular shape and jagged edges. Even though these particles are different in size and shape, they flow harmoniously through the universe and our body's systems (e.g., nervous, circulatory, digestive, muscular, etc.). They are the energies of creation. They are "potential."

Every number is composed of both positive and negative energy. A number's energy manifests in behavior as energetic patterns of choice. Positive energy is focused energy. It seeks the most direct route to its destination by flowing through, over, or around the obstructions it encounters along its path. Positive behavior patterns reflect conscious choices. Negative energy, in this instance, is unfocused energy. Unfocused energy is much like a stream that meanders across the landscape, avoiding the obstacles in its path. By not choosing a direction, the stream chooses to lengthen its journey by reacting to its environment. The intensity of our negative/reactive behavior patterns is a reflection of the depth of our abandonment anxieties. Every time we do something to be loved or to maintain control, we pump one additional particle of negative energy into our bodies. As the proportion of negative particles increases, so does the probability of developing health issues and nurturing negative behavior patterns.

Unless you are satisfied with just reading the number interpretations from the book, I cannot emphasize enough the importance of taking the time to learn the subtleties of the positive and negative interpretations of the numbers 1 through 9. Numbers are a language that can provide answers to all of your questions. Learning any new language takes time and practice. Be kind and patient with yourself.

TABLE OF POSITIVE AND NEGATIVE
ATTRIBUTES OF NUMBERS

1 • Issues of the Ego Self

Positive: Self-directed, leader, paradigm buster, innovator, assertive, energetic, balanced, follows internal guidance, an initiator, comfortable with self

Negative: Passive, aggressive, egocentric, low self-esteem, fearful, timid, arrogant, a zealot, a bully, no sense of self

2 • Issues Involving Others

Positive: Sensitive, intuitive, cooperative, a mediator/arbitrator, organizer, harmonizer, friendly, communicates in timely fashion, detail oriented, tactful, loyal, has a good voice

Negative: Subservient, shy, overly sentimental, timid, careless about "things," codependent, does not speak up for self, self-centered, difficulty letting go of emotional and sentimental attachments, blunt, insensitive, has difficulty working with others—not a team player, hides emotions, could be nonverbal, may beat people with the "hammer of truth"

3 • Issues Involving Communication, Social Interactions, Feelings of Inadequacy

Positive: Joyful, witty, artistic, charismatic, charming, creative, intelligent, optimistic, communicative, extroverted, visionary, musical, good sense of humor—likes to laugh

Negative: Moody/emotional, unforgiving, scattered, introverted, exaggerates, vain, feelings of inferiority or inadequacy, leaves things unfinished, sarcastic, grandiose plans, jealous, concerned about being judged, temperamental, ill-tempered, a bit of a gossip

4 • Issues Involving Details and "Getting Things Done"

Positive: Organized, an architect, a builder, systematic, logical, dependable, practical, a manager, ability to totally focus on a task, a logician

1	2	3	4	5	6	7	8	9
A	B	C	D	E	F	G	H	I
J	K	L	M	N	O	P	Q	R
S	T	U	V	W	X	Y	Z	

14   Cosmic Numerology and Quantum Numbers

Negative: Prejudicial, a reactionary, a procrastinator, unimaginative, gets lost in minutiae, stubborn, goes "by the book," confrontational, dull, hides in logic, can be hateful

5 • Issues Involving Change and Movement

Positive: Flexible, freedom loving, physical, enjoys life, loves innovation and change, curious, can be moderate, balanced, easily goes with the flow

Negative: Unbalanced—too rigid or too yielding, impulsive, self-indulgent, inconsistent, promiscuous, indulges to excess, deals with concepts not details, always in a hurry

6 • Issues Involving Family, Community, Relationships, Responsibility

Positive: Responsible, an advisor/counselor/mentor, protector, nurturer, humanitarian, service oriented, domestic, compassionate

Negative: A perfectionist, a martyr, nosy, overly protective, a giver of unsought advice, codependent, avoids obligations/commitments/relationships/responsibility, needs to be in control

7 • Issues Involving Abandonment, Trust, Skepticism, and Control

Positive: Trusting, spiritual, intuitive, psychic, introspective, empathetic, objective, open, vulnerable, a seeker of knowledge, patient, insightful, analytical, can see all sides of an issue

Negative: Controlling, fearful, distrustful, impatient, emotionally closed, mental or emotional paralysis from being overly analytical, socially/emotionally disconnected, a zealot, a martyr, messianic feelings, codependent—a need to be needed

8 • Issues Involving Power, Money, Control, and Status

Positive: Initiates/delegates/orchestrates, logical, likes to be in charge, a natural leader, makes it happen, good at politics/business/commerce/leading institutions or organizations, "walks the talk," looks good in any kind of attire, possesses knowledge, wisdom, and expertise

Negative: Easily frustrated, temperamental, extravagant/cheap, dictatorial, stubborn, materialistic, demands recognition, mean, a bully, fearful of using personal power, can be disloyal if he or she feels slighted or ignored, has a fear of success, whatever money comes is always needed for higher than expected expenses, may tend to avoid the world of business and commerce but complain about not having enough money

9 • Issues Involving Selflessness

Positive: Selfless, loves unconditionally, compassionate, embraces brotherhood, a natural actor, loves long-distance travel, comfortable with all strata of society, works to raise the level of self-awareness on the planet, has let go of ego issues and embraced the higher Self

Negative: Egotistical, needs recognition/appreciation/thanks for "good deeds," has difficulty letting go, can be fearful of showing any emotion, can be emotionally isolated or codependent, can be an "emotional pin cushion" (i.e., holds the emotions and feelings of others like a reservoir holds water)

0 • Issues Related to Spirit

A zero (0) attached to any number indicates the availability of *direct* spiritual assistance; when that energy is used in a positive manner, it's like a turbo boost. For example, the number 10 indicates assistance with endeavors involving beginnings and leadership. The number 102 could indicate assistance in individual projects (1) that would be of benefit to or require the assistance of others (2).

2

Achievement Numbers and Core Issues in Life

Your achievement number (AN) reveals your core issues; it is the hub of your numerological chart, from which all other numbers radiate like the spokes of a wheel.* Until you become aware of and resolve the issues associated with your achievement number, its negative aspects will rule your life. If, for example, your achievement number is a 3, you must learn to overcome feelings of insecurity, inadequacy, and inferiority, and tendencies toward scatteredness, exaggeration, gossiping, and grandiosity by becoming proficient at something. Whether it's flipping pancakes or performing brain surgery, if you feel/know that you are the best at what you do, then the feelings of inadequacy and insecurity will dissolve and never return. It is at this point that the achievement number rotates from negative to positive and becomes your greatest strength.

---

*Although I've never seen it in a copyrighted format, to the best of my knowledge, the original achievement number concept was developed by Kevin Quinn Avery. I have simplified and modified the process.

HOW TO DETERMINE YOUR ACHIEVEMENT NUMBER

To determine your achievement number, add together the numbers for your month and day of birth. Write down the sum. For example: if your birthday is March 4, add together 3 + 4 for an achievement number of 7.

If the number is a double digit, write the sum of those two numbers following the original sum. For example, if your birthday is October 8, add together 10 + 8 = 18, then reduce it to a single digit by adding 1 + 8 = 9. Your achievement number is 9, which is written as 18/9. The number is written in this way because the underlying double-digit number can also be used to identify subtle aspects of your achievement number. Taking both the double digit and its sum into consideration will give you a more complete understanding of your behavior patterns.

If the first addition of two digits again results in a double digit, continue adding the numbers together until you get a single digit. For example, if your birthday is April 24: 4 + 24 = 28, 2 + 8 = 10, and 1 + 0 = 1. You would then write your achievement number as 28/1.

> **Note:** When figuring your achievement number, use the birth date on your birth certificate or the date of your court-approved name change. The reason for using the court date as your new birthday is that the choice of a new name is also a choice to be reborn, which brings in a new set of challenges.

SIMPLE INTERPRETATION OF ACHIEVEMENT NUMBERS

You can use the basic number concepts, along with their fundamental positive and negative aspects, given in chapter 1, to do a simple

```
1 2 3 4 5 6 7 8 9
A B C D E F G H I
J K L M N O P Q R
S T U V W X Y Z
```

18   Achievement Numbers and Core Issues in Life

interpretation of your or another person's achievement number. Below are sample interpretations of achievement numbers, using just these numeric concepts.

March 4   3 + 4 = 7   AN = 7

Positive: Letting go of control and skepticism (7), making things happen (4) leads to improved communication and social interactions (3).

Negative: This individual has difficulty completing things (4) due to feelings of inadequacy (3) associated with trust, skepticism, and control (7).

February 28   2 + 28 = 30   3 + 0 = 3   AN = 30/3

Positive: Accepting spiritual assistance (0) enhances creativity and creates more positive social interactions (3), resulting in a visionary who can make his or her visions into reality.

Negative: Poor communication and social skills (3) associated with feelings of inadequacy (3).

Determine and Interpret Achievement Numbers

Practice determining and interpreting your achievement number and those of a few people known to you by referring to the *Table of Basic Number Concepts* and the *Table of Positive and Negative Attributes of Numbers,* given in chapter 1.

Sample:

Month 10 + day 8 = 18   Reduce if necessary: 1 + 8 = 9

The achievement number is: 18/9

The core issues are: 9—control and codependency; 8—lack of self-empowerment or being a bully; 1—lack of confidence can make them timid or arrogant

Month ____ + day ____ = ____   Reduce if necessary: _____

The achievement number is: _____

The core issues are:

Month _____ + day _____ = _____   Reduce if necessary: _____
The achievement number is: _____
The core issues are:

Month _____ + day _____ = _____   Reduce if necessary: _____
The achievement number is: _____
The core issues are:

DETAILED DESCRIPTIONS OF THE
ACHIEVEMENT NUMBERS

The following descriptions of the achievement numbers encompass both extremes of behavior patterns, that is, having too much or too little of some aspect of the self. Keep in mind that it is rare for a person to display all of the negative aspects associated with a number. Once you recognize and resolve the negative aspects of your achievement number, it will represent your greatest strength and you will embody the positive qualities, also shown below.

Achievement Number 1 • Low self-esteem is the main issue, which can sometimes appear as arrogance or bullying rather than timidity. Some individuals with this achievement number may be confrontational toward authority, while others may be withdrawn. If your achievement

20   Achievement Numbers and Core Issues in Life

1	2	3	4	5	6	7	8	9
A	B	C	D	E	F	G	H	I
J	K	L	M	N	O	P	Q	R
S	T	U	V	W	X	Y	Z	

number is 1, you must learn to stand on your own and not let others define your identity or make your decisions. You will encounter situations that will test your courage and faith.

Positive: Centered, confident, innovative, a paradigm shifter, leader, and explorer.

Achievement Number 2 • The key word for anyone whose achievement number is 2 is *balance.* The main issues are not speaking up in a timely fashion, being overly sensitive or insensitive, being too timid or too blunt, anxieties over commitment, shyness, and codependency. If your achievement number is 2, you need to learn not to base your identity on how others perceive you. A negative 2 also needs to learn to let go of things (there is a tendency to hold on for sentimental or emotional reasons); pay more attention to details; and practice tact, cooperation, and getting along with feminine energy (i.e., energy coming from the heart instead of the head, whether in a man or a woman). Speaking up in a timely manner can also be an issue. Those for whom speaking up is not an issue need to put a little padding on the end of their hammer of truth and learn to compromise, to create win-win situations.

Those with this achievement number may have poor posture if they have a habit of drooping their arms and legs over chairs or other objects while talking on the telephone or watching television. A person with this achievement number who has difficulty interacting with others can become a couch potato.

Positive: Speaks up in a timely fashion; is a harmonizer, mediator, arbitrator, and delegator (has learned "I cannot do it all myself").

Achievement Number 3 • The main issues are overcoming a lack of emotional intimacy and feelings of insecurity, inferiority, inadequacy, or scatteredness. If you have an achievement number of 3 you may have trouble keeping your word because of the tendency to overobligate. Sarcasm may also be an issue. You may dazzle people with your creativity, charm, charisma, and intelligence but will rarely finish what you start because you don't want to be judged. (If you were given a dime each time someone told you "what great potential you have," you could retire!) To overcome feelings of inadequacy the solution is to focus on fewer projects, to gain mastery, and to finish what is started. It doesn't matter if it is a vocation or avocation. Because we are all unique, when we act to the best of our ability from moment to moment, that makes us the best in the world at what we do. Along with that it is important to learn to communicate either orally or in writing, to temper sarcasm, and to be more forgiving of both self and others.

Positive: Joyful, charming, creative, intelligent, optimistic, a communicator, extrovert, visionary, and musician, good sense of humor.

Achievement Number 4 • Control is a major issue for this achievement number, as is procrastination. These individuals can be workaholics. They like order, system, and structure. If you have an achievement number 4, you need to learn not to be overly logical and get stuck in the minutiae of going "by the book" (your own book). You might have confrontations with authority, feeling you should be the boss. A negative 4 can also be a reactionary, someone that fights change, embracing the motto, "If it ain't broke, don't fix it." Change challenges this kind of person's belief systems, which they cling to, fearful of being left without an anchor. The main challenges are to build a solid foundation and to avoid taking shortcuts, procrastinating, and being judgmental, stubborn, or prejudicial.

Positive: Well organized, with the ability to get things done and a natural affinity for form, fit, and function, knowing how to put things together (like architects, builders, planners).

Achievement Number 5 • This number represents a desire for freedom, the freedom to do what you want, when you want, with whom you want, any time you want, anywhere you want, for as long as you want. Even though those with number 5 want this freedom of choice, they usually don't have the courage to pursue that freedom. Or their

1	2	3	4	5	6	7	8	9
A	B	C	D	E	F	G	H	I
J	K	L	M	N	O	P	Q	R
S	T	U	V	W	X	Y	Z	

22   Achievement Numbers and Core Issues in Life

behavior patterns can reflect overindulgence, a tendency to lose interest quickly or to get a concept but not focus on the details. In life and as drivers they can be somewhat reckless and speed loving. They can become either adventurers seeking out life or voyeurs running from life. Any major decisions impulsively made seldom work to their benefit.

If your achievement number is 5, you may sometimes be overly flexible in trying to satisfy others; at other times you can be so rigid and inflexible you need to have someone put liniment on your back so that you can get out of bed. If that is the case, you will always have a *go slow/go fast, too little/too much* quality on the physical plane, until both internal and external balance is achieved. You need to learn moderation of the senses and balance. Individuals with an achievement number of 5 can expect life changes to occur every twelve to eighteen months. Those with this achievement number must learn to accept the transitory nature of life: one day even Mt. Everest, six miles of solid rock, will be nothing but grains of sand on the beaches of an unnamed ocean.

Positive: Moderate in all actions (mental, physical, emotional, and spiritual), flexible, with the capacity to be in the moment and to accept change as inevitable. Freedom loving and has developed skills to support that freedom.

Achievement Number 6 • Whether male or female, if you have this achievement number, you like to be the "mother hen," yet don't always want the responsibility unless you are given the authority to make decisions, because you don't want to take the heat for someone else's mistakes. You have a tendency to try to do too much, for too many, with too little, and then see yourself as a failure. At the other end of the spectrum is a pattern of irresponsibility. Then your challenge is to learn to accept responsibility, first for yourself, and then to responsibly be of service to family and community. You need to learn not to be an emotional buffer for others. This includes easing back from unrealistic expectations and perfectionist tendencies.

As a result of unrealistic expectations and perfectionist tendencies, many school-age children with this achievement number appear to make little or no attempt at mastering their academic subjects; the underlying reason is that they would rather be called lazy than stupid.

Positive: Responsible, an advisor/counselor/mentor (who does not give advice but instead asks questions that lead another to an insight or revelation), a protector, nurturer, humanitarian, service oriented, domestic, compassionate.

Achievement Number 7 • Abandonment issues are a primary factor influencing the way those with this achievement number interact with others. If you have an achievement number of 7, you have a need to be needed or validated for your wisdom, intelligence, compassion, insights, or usefulness. It is much easier for you to give than receive; you may find it very hard to open up and be vulnerable. Even though those with this achievement number are usually reserved, at times they can be outrageous, a maneuver that allows them to size up a situation and plan their next move. They have major concerns about making a mistake and being embarrassed, humiliated, or having people think they are not as good as they know they are. This is one reason they can be perceived as being somewhat aloof.

For those with an achievement number of 7, patience is a huge issue: you have very little, if any. The opposite is also true; you may get bogged down overanalyzing minutiae because of your need to avoid the embarrassment of not knowing. You need to know and will ask lots of questions. What you cannot learn from questioning, you will attempt to find out by "hook or crook," that is, prying with whatever means is necessary.

The challenge for those with this achievement number is to stop trying to be the teacher or healer by offering unsought advice or telling others what they need to do (thinking such advice will help them avoid pain and suffering). This only creates frustration when they don't listen, and feeds into a sense of being different, isolated, or ignored. Above all else a person with this achievement number must learn faith and patience and that the universe unfolds according to a Cosmic Plan. Personal desires (based on abandonment issues) have to be subjugated and the universe allowed to unfold as it will. You also need to avoid engaging in purposeless activity—doing something out of boredom or loneliness—as it will only lead to negative consequences.

Positive: Trusting, spiritual, analytical, psychic, introspective, empathetic, objective, open, vulnerable, a seeker of knowledge, patient, insightful, intuitive, can see all sides of an issue. The positive 7 has learned, "I have not been abandoned, control is an illusion, all things come to those with patience, I am not the messiah, and it is not my job to save anyone." Most importantly, the positive 7 has learned to strengthen his or her relationship with the god energy.

Achievement Number 8 • Money is a major issue for those with this achievement number: you can spend money like a drunken sailor or squeeze a dollar so hard that tears come to George's eyes. You can have a fear of success or be driven to achieve it, regardless of the personal costs. You can become frustrated if you feel you are not being given the recognition you deserve, which may lead to disloyalty. You may have issues with authority. Individuals with this achievement number can be arrogant or a bully. They can have a very short fuse. For those with this achievement number, there is always the possibility of violence in speech, action, or manner, either as a perpetrator or victim.

The challenge for those with the achievement number 8 is to prove their superiority, not demand it, by using their innate wisdom, knowledge, and expertise to demonstrate their leadership abilities. They need to stop trying to do everything themselves, feeling that others are unreliable or untrustworthy. They need to develop true humanitarian feelings, not just those of an opportunist, and to not depend solely on their logic but to learn to trust their intuition as well.

Positive: A leader, not a manager, who has the ability and bearing to organize, orchestrate, and delegate to others; good at politics/business/commerce/leading institutions or organizations; "walks the talk"; looks good in any kind of attire; possesses knowledge, wisdom, and expertise.

Achievement Number 9 • The individuals who have 9 as an achievement number have chosen to take a final exam on being human. In addition to the challenge of 9 itself (learning to do what you love, rather than trying to be loved or to maintain control), there are challenges associated with each of the previous eight challenges: issues involving the ego self, others, communication and focus, overcoming procrastination and control issues, learning to be flexible, balancing responsibility, overcoming impatience and abandonment issues, and not being afraid to lead.

There are three potential behavior patterns for those with a 9 achievement number. In no specific order:

- Having resolved their abandonment illusion and developed the courage to do what they love, they have chosen to proactively live their life calling.
- Thriving on the drama of life, they are natural actors who can fake emotions. They have a need to control others based on the perception that they are responsible for everyone's success or survival. These are people who will pour out their hearts to anyone who will listen.
- This group has codependency issues. It is very difficult, if not impossible, for them to release emotional attachments, whether they are memories, possessions, relationships, or feelings.

Positive: Compassionate, able to give unconditional love; able to deal with emotions and to use life experiences to help others; able to be of service with no thought of recognition, appreciation, or thanks—to do for others because it brings joy; have let go of the past and embraced the future; able to "be in the world but not attached to it."

MASTER NUMBERS AND KARMIC NUMBERS

There are two special categories of numbers: master numbers (11, 22, 33, and other multiples of 11 through 99) and karmic numbers (13, 14, 16, and 19). Notice that each of these special numbers is preceded by a 1, which indicates issues involving the ego. When your birth date equation includes one of these numbers, it represents more intense challenges than other number combinations. For example, a birth date of June 5 would be 6 + 5 = 11 and 1 + 1 = 2, resulting in an achievement number of 11/2, which includes the master number 11; May 8 would be 5 + 8 = 13 and 1 + 3 = 4, resulting in an achievement number of 13/4, which includes the karmic number 13. If your birth date equation includes a master or karmic number, then you should refer to the description of that number given below as well as to the description of its reduced single digit.

Descriptions of the Master Numbers

When a master number appears, it signals an opportunity for rapid growth by recognizing how your abandonment issues are influencing your behavior patterns. Negative master numbers can be very difficult to work with if you are still wrestling with the illusion that you know more than god and are waiting for the opportunity to prove it. Being composed of two identical single digits, a master number doubles the negative aspects, resulting in a more powerful influence. An individual with master numbers is being called on to perform at a higher level of consciousness than most others. If you avoid, ignore, abuse, or misuse your special talents, you will always encounter obstacles to your success. Your master number will become a master challenge.

Although the master numbers range from 11 to 99, I'll only describe three master numbers (11, 22, 33) because the highest achievement number is 43/7, based on a December 31 birthday.

Master Number 11 • This number indicates a challenge that can involve a sense of self-righteousness, hypersensitivity to others or the environment, or zealousness attached to a belief or cause. It brings the knowledge of how things could be and a frustration that you are given neither the power nor the opportunity to make them that way. At one extreme are zealots who willingly sacrifice themselves for a belief or cause; at the other end of the spectrum are idealists who have lost all hope of making a mass societal change and withdraw or become isolated from life.

A person whose birth date equation is 11/2 is influenced by the positive and negative vibrations of both the 1 and 2 achievement numbers, since two ones (11) added together create the sum of 2. This can result in conflicting behavior patterns. A person with the negative aspects of 2 can be shy, timid, and noncommunicative, or uncooperative, brutally blunt, insensitive, uncooperative, and uncompromising. A negative 2 is influenced and shaded by the negative 1 (lack of confidence, low self-esteem, stubbornly doing it their way, arrogant). Big issues with a negative 2 pattern are learning to release emotional or sentimental attachments to thoughts, memories, material possessions, and codependency. If you are presented with this challenge, you need to forget about making a BIG difference and be content with just making a difference.

Positive: A person who exhibits the positive elements of the number 1, doubled, will be self-confident, assured, centered, conscious, and aware of his or her environment. Such an individual will be able to speak up in a timely manner, trust intuition, facilitate mutual cooperation, and be in partnership with Spirit. The positive 11/2 has established a working partnership (2) with the god energy. Kind, caring, thoughtful, intuitive, and empathetic, harmonizers and facilitators, they make good partners and are always willing to do their share. The positive 2 with an excellent voice has the potential to reach people's hearts through singing or speaking.

28   Achievement Numbers and Core Issues in Life

```
1 2 3 4 5 6 7 8 9
A B C D E F G H I
J K L M N O P Q R
S T U V W X Y Z
```

Master Number 22 • This number also carries the characteristics of the 2 and 4 achievement numbers. The double 2s indicate there are two main patterns; the first is a need for preapproval (in order to avoid rejection). A high level of sensitivity to the inputs of others can create situations where the 22 would give up rather than fight for what he or she believes in (negative 2 behavior patterns). As an example, a woman who lives alone decides to landscape her backyard. She enthusiastically sketches out where she wants to place the fountains, flowers, hedges, and walkways. When she shows the sketch to two friends, the first says, "It's a waste of money, you'll never get your investment back when you sell your house." The second says, "You already work 55 hours a week, when will you have the time to work on your garden? You're wasting your time!" Having been told by two "friends" that it was a bad idea, the 22 listens to them instead of to what is in her heart. This is the preapproval dilemma of the 22.

The other pattern can be a tendency to be somewhat confrontational with superiors and authority figures because a 22 is ultimately a 4, leading the person to feel that he has worked out all of the details and has the perfect plan, which should be accepted by others on faith alone. If it isn't, he can become defensive. As part of the 2 energy, these individuals may have difficulty with others because they find it hard to let go of emotional or sentimental attachments, including attachments to their own ideas. The energy of 4 makes such a person cling to his beliefs. It's all tied in with abandonment issues.

A technique that a 22 can use to minimize confrontations (i.e., pushing people's buttons), especially with those in authority, is to eliminate using the word *change* and use the word *modify* instead. Whenever the word *change* is used, it becomes a challenge to the person being asked to do it. This activates abandonment issues. Using the word *modify* implies that something is working and if it is modified, it will work better. This is a win-win statement. The authority does not feel challenged, and the 22 doesn't feel ignored.

Positive: A person with this master number has a logical mind and pays attention to details. Such a person can be a great organizer, builder, or architect, with the potential to make a difference on a global level: to put tunnels through mountains, run a multinational corporation, carve cities out of jungles, build roads across deserts, or start a new religion.

Master Number 33 • This number also carries the characteristics of the 3 and 6 achievement numbers. That results in the person being challenged to avoid negative 3 traits, such as feelings of inadequacy, scatteredness, difficulties with being emotionally intimate (speaking heartfelt truths), being a social introvert, or having a misplaced sense of obligation, duty, and responsibility. Under the heading of "codependent personality patterns," a person with this master number would be classified as a *doer,* an individual who volunteers to do everything for everyone, thus making herself indispensible. This pattern can be directly linked to the depth of her abandonment issues. It is very easy for such a person to take on responsibilities that should be shouldered by others. The influence of 6 can result in being weighed down by unrealistic expectations and perfectionist tendencies directed to self or others. Examples of this could be:

- Students with a 6 as part of their achievement number will begin projects enthusiastically but appear to lose interest rather quickly. One reason is they get frustrated that they cannot keep up with their expectations of success. Not wanting to appear "stupid" in the eyes of others, they adopt a pattern of indifference or laziness.
- Someone who is perceived as being responsible for the success of others (such as a manager, teacher, therapist, or parent) tries to guarantee his own success by attempting to get his charges to do things his way.
- Someone who is constantly poking her nose into other people's business and offering unsolicited advice.

Because of unrealistic expectations and apprehension, or an inability to speak up, a person with this master number may have an emotional "blow up," which seems to come from nowhere, over a seemingly inconsequential word, event, or act.

Positive: With excellent communication and mentoring skills, a charismatic personality, and deep, universal insights, a person with this number can become a master teacher/healer/mentor to the world at large.

Descriptions of the Karmic Numbers

Like the master numbers, karmic numbers are double-digit numbers that bring their negative aspects with them. Karmic numbers are unlearned life lessons sitting on the head of a pin. We can either avoid the pinprick by taking conscious action or allow ourselves to react to the prick. Three numbers combine to form each karmic number. For example, 13 combines the negative and positive aspects of 1, 3, and 4.

Karmic Number 13 • This number represents a karmic challenge that can result in laziness or procrastination, indicating a reticence to "let go"—transitions are difficult to make due to feelings of inadequacy (3) and low self-esteem (1). When opportunities are presented that would help such individuals develop the confidence to begin making their dreams and visions into reality, they may or may not pursue them; it all depends on the depth of their feelings of inadequacy and low self-esteem.

Individuals with this karmic number have a tendency at times to be very unforgiving, sarcastic, skeptical, controlling, stubborn, and reactionary. They find it difficult, and at times outright refuse, to accept advice or guidance from others. As an example, a person with a 13 karmic number is at the end of a long hallway heading for the elevator when he sees the elevator doors open and two people exiting the elevator. However, when he is about fifteen feet away from the elevator, a maintenance worker places an "Out of Order" sign on the elevator doors and turns and walks away. The individual with the 13 karmic number thinks it may be a trick or that the sign was placed on the wrong elevator. After all, two people just exited the elevator! He pushes the elevator button and, when it opens, steps in and pushes the down button. The elevator travels about thirteen feet and then stops and its interior lights go out; the 13 is stuck between floors.

Positive: A person with this karmic number can be a visionary (3) who makes innovative ideas (1) into realities (4).

Karmic Number 14 • This is a challenge number that indicates the person is out of balance, either too flexible or too rigid. A person with this number can also be stubborn (4) due to a lack of confidence (1), which can make him or her difficult to deal with. With the 14, "if some is good, more is better; if more is better, then back up that truck loaded with 'excesses' and dump it at my door!" Those excesses may be displayed as behavior that involves immersion in or aversion to food, drugs, drink, sex, gambling, and so on. This is an energy that can result in "pushing the envelope," such as participating in extreme sports or being argumentative.

This number also carries the negative characteristics of the 1, 4, and 5 achievement numbers. There are two different ways to interpret this number; one way is to analyze what makes people with this number rigid, and the other is to analyze what makes them impulsive.

- A rigid 1, 4, 5 pattern: The lack of confidence and low self-esteem (1) are the catalysts for procrastination, stubbornness, a desire for a "pre-guarantee" before taking action, using biased logic to avoid tasks, or taking a reactionary stance (4). This pattern makes it difficult for the 5 to open to change or movement.
- An impulsive 1, 4, 5 pattern: Overconfidence (1), a tendency to ignore the details (4), and an attitude of being entitled to do what they want, when they want, for as long as they want (5).

Positive: A person with this karmic number has a practical (4) and innovative approach (1) along with the confidence (1) that provides her with the ability to either flow with life's changes or implement them (5).

Karmic Number 16 • This karmic challenge number indicates the possibility of catastrophe or loss if the person goes against an intuitive prompting or tries to maintain control. This number also carries the characteristics of the negative 1, 6, and 7 achievement numbers. With this number, a person will have a tendency to follow his head and not his heart; to rationalize, intellectualize, and justify. He will try to figure out everything "a hundred different ways from Sunday"; his biggest anxiety is not getting it right and being blamed, embarrassed, or humiliated and then abandoned for his perceived lack of value. This is why a 16/7 tries so hard. Believe it or not, this individual is right 99.999999999 percent of the time, but not 100 percent of the time. This means he is not god, and therefore must learn to refrain from telling everyone what *they* need to do, how to do it, and when.

A person with this number desperately wants to be recognized for her wisdom, insights, and contributions to a group. As much as she wants to belong, she is fearful of betrayal, embarrassment, humiliation, and abandonment, and so remains outside with her nose pressed against the windowpane, looking in. Such a person feels hurt, rejected, or unappreciated when her unsolicited advice is rejected, ignored, or laughed at. To rectify this situation, she will have a closet full of various size hammers, from large to stupendous, to use as she tries to try to pound square pegs into round holes, that is, to make things *right for her.*

A person with 16/7 can be overly concerned for the welfare of others, even to the point of messianic behavior, because he believes his advice can save everyone from pain and suffering. Such a person ignores the point made by Herman Hesse in his book *Siddhartha:* "You can die ten thousand times for someone and not be able to alter their destiny." The 16/7 person does not believe that message because of his messianic need to save everyone, such as in the following example: There is a catastrophe on the way, a tidal wave, forest fire, avalanche, or flood. The 16/7 rushes to the edge of town, plants his feet, takes a deep breath, and then holds out his hands to stop whatever is coming, but is instead killed. From the celestial realm, he looks down and is angered and disappointed that no one knows of his sacrifice or even cares. He wanted to be seen as a savior and be given a "no cut contract." He wanted to hear, "Thank you for saving us; what would we have done without you?"

A person with 16/7 is standing on the side of the road as a man comes through town weighed down by a cross, which Roman soldiers are forcing him to carry. He runs over and says, "Let me carry your cross," and takes it on his shoulders. A little farther down the road, he encounters a man beating his donkey because it refuses to carry a heavy load of oil. The 16/7 person says, "Stop beating that animal, I'll carry your casks of oil," and puts them on his back. The weight almost makes his knees buckle, but he moves forward. A little farther down the road, he sees a woman yelling at and beating her two children. He commands her to stop and asks her why she is doing this. She replies, "They are worthless, just two more mouths to feed; I should drown them in the river." He says, "I'll take them, give them to me, I'll raise them like they were my own children." He lifts up the children, placing one in each arm, takes ten steps, then collapses and dies from a heart attack. The woman takes her children back, the owner of the donkey reties the casks of oil onto the donkey's back, and the Roman soldiers make the man pick up his cross and continue carrying it. The person with 16/7, wishing to prevent others from suffering pain or making mistakes, interfered with their destinies, thinking he knew best, and it cost him his life. Plus nobody cared about him or what he was trying to do.

The opposite can also be true. A person with this number can be irresponsible (6), with low self-esteem (1) and emotionally disconnected (7), choosing to live by her own rules, because of a fear that things will not work the way they are "supposed to" and she will be embarrassed or humiliated. Or the dynamics of 1, 6, and 7 can result in situations like the following: while a woman is buying a used car, a voice inside says "pass it up," but she ignores it because she likes the color or the stereo system, wants to impress someone, feels sorry for the seller, or doesn't want to appear to be wasting the salesperson's time.

Positive: Someone who provides a unique service to humanity (6) by creating new paradigms (1) with the information he receives from Source (7).

Karmic Number 19 • This number also carries the negative characteristics of the 1 and 9 achievement numbers. It usually indicates there can be pain and suffering during the first twenty years of life (9). The pain can be mental, emotional, physical, or spiritual; its purpose is to prepare these individuals, as potential leaders in their fields, to develop a stronger sense of self (1). The way we develop a stronger sense of self is to stop looking over our shoulders (9) and start looking over the rainbow. Who better to lead than someone whose life experiences have taught him determination, persistence, and compassion, and given him a more worldly view (9)?

A 19/1 achievement number can indicate behavior patterns that can swing between loving, compassionate, and understanding (9) to merciless (1). The merciless aspect is linked with control issues (9), which stem from cosmic abandonment issues. The illusion is, "If I (1) control things, everything will be fine (9)."

Many with this karmic number may have a tendency to do for others as an excuse for not doing for themselves. A lack of confidence or low self-esteem (1) coupled with a need to be loved (9) combine to form a codependent behavior pattern. The opposite pattern would be demonstrated by people who are egotistical (1), flamboyant (9), and starstruck with themselves; they care for nothing but themselves and what they want, and won't let anything get in their way.

Positive: Having recognized and eliminated abandonment issues and developed the confidence to make self the first priority (1), by doing what she loves (9), this individual is ready to assume a leadership role.

3

Finding Soulutions to Achievement Number Challenges

The numbers we choose for our date of birth identify both our life's challenges and their soulutions. These choices include challenges as gentle as a caress (loss of recess in first grade) or as harsh as a 40-ton steel I-beam between the eyes (terminal illness, laid off at 55). Every achievement number challenge has a soulution; every negative influence can be counteracted. The soulution is usually to *do less of one thing* and *more of another* or vice versa. For example, you can either be totally insensitive to the needs of others or overly sensitive to the needs of others; in either case, there is a need for balance. It is the same with our bodies: they need to be balanced. When they aren't, we become susceptible to illness, disease, and physical injury.

Through Cosmic Numerology it is possible to chart the soulution associated with each achievement number challenge. This chart is a "Rosetta stone" that can help you decipher your reactive behavior patterns (or those of others) and the conscious, proactive choices that will amend them. In order to use the chart, you need to begin with a *personal number:* a total derived from adding or subtracting a series

1	2	3	4	5	6	7	8	9
A	B	C	D	E	F	G	H	I
J	K	L	M	N	O	P	Q	R
S	T	U	V	W	X	Y	Z	

of numbers associated with anything that involves you (or the person you are interested in), such as your achievement number, your name, health issues, phone numbers, addresses, cravings, feelings, emotions, dreams, impulsive behaviors, colors, ideas, injuries, license plate numbers, and so on. The personal numbers of corporations, businesses, governments, countries, political parties, or animals can also be interpreted.

In the next chapter, we will examine the challenges associated with a person's given name in greater detail; for the purposes of this analysis, any name, whether of a person, a behavior, an emotion, or whatever, can be simply converted using the chart below.

LETTER–TO–NUMBER CONVERSION

In order to convert a name to a number, you need to use the classical conversion chart used to transpose letters into their numeric equivalents, shown below. In the chart the vowels are shown in bold. (I include the letters *W* and *Y* as vowels along with the traditional vowels *A, E, I, O,* and *U.*)

Letter-to-Number Conversion Chart

1	2	3	4	5	6	7	8	9
A	B	C	D	**E**	F	G	H	**I**
J	K	L	M	N	**O**	P	Q	R
S	T	U	V	**W**	X	**Y**	Z	

The Math

When you add the numeric total of all the letters in a word or series of words, you will usually get a multi-digit number. Just as with the birth

date, the numbers are always reduced to a single digit. They are similarly written with both the single-digit and the double-digit numbers,
as the individual numbers that make up a two- or three-digit number
identify underlying energies. Practice converting a few words into their
numeric equivalents and then consult the *Table of Positive and Negative
Attributes of Numbers* in chapter 1 (pages 13–15) to see how the positive and negative interpretations of the numbers match the energy of
the word. For example, *love* adds up to 18, is reduced to 9 (1 + 8 = 9),
and is written as 18/9. True love, a positive 9, deals with selflessness.
Negative 9 would be egotistical.

IDENTIFYING THE SOULUTIONS TO YOUR LIFE'S CHALLENGES

After having derived your achievement number (see chapter 2) and a
personal number related to a significant aspect of behavior, emotional
reaction, circumstance, and so on (for yourself or others), use the table
below to find the soulution related to that specific challenge. This chart
can be used to better understand why people behave the way they do
as well as to provide specific guidance for living a more proactive life.
It lays out the 162 behavior patterns of the basic human personality
matrix. Each personality has nine aspects, and each of those aspects is
composed of nine reactive behavior patterns (shown on the line marked
"**Challenge**") and nine conscious proactive choice patterns (shown on
the line marked "*Soulution*"). Our reactive behavior patterns originate
with our abandonment issues. Living the soulution pattern is our road
map to the land of abundance.

Begin by locating the personal number you have derived in the sec-
tion below devoted to your (or another person's) achievement number.
For example, for a person whose achievement number is 1, the personal
number **5** has a **9** challenge with an **8** soulution (see chart). It would
be written as a proper number 5 with a fraction 9/8 (5 9/8). The top

number of the fraction is always the challenge and the bottom number is always the soulution.

TABLE OF CHALLENGES AND SOULUTIONS

Achievement Number 1

Personal Number	1 2 3 4 **5** 6 7 8 9
Challenge	1 3 5 7 **9** 2 4 6 8
Soulution	9 2 4 6 **8** 1 3 5 7

Achievement Number 2

Personal Number	1 2 3 4 5 6 7 8 9
Challenge	9 2 4 6 8 1 3 5 7
Soulution	7 9 2 4 6 8 1 3 5

Achievement Number 3

Personal Number	1 2 3 4 5 6 7 8 9
Challenge	8 1 3 5 7 9 2 4 6
Soulution	5 7 9 2 4 6 8 1 3

Achievement Number 4

Personal Number	1 2 3 4 5 6 7 8 9
Challenge	7 9 2 4 6 8 1 3 5
Soulution	3 5 7 9 2 4 6 8 1

Achievement Number 5

Personal Number	1 2 3 4 5 6 7 8 9
Challenge	6 8 1 3 5 7 9 2 4
Soulution	1 3 5 7 9 2 4 6 8

Achievement Number 6

Personal Number	1 2 3 4 5 6 7 8 9
Challenge	5 7 9 2 4 6 8 1 3
Soulution	8 1 3 5 7 9 2 4 6

Achievement Number 7

Personal Number	1 2 3 4 5 6 7 8 9
Challenge	4 6 8 1 3 5 7 9 2
Soulution	6 8 1 3 5 7 9 2 4

Achievement Number 8

Personal Number	1 2 3 4 5 6 7 8 9
Challenge	3 5 7 9 2 4 6 8 1
Soulution	4 6 8 1 3 5 7 9 2

Achievement Number 9

Personal Number	1 2 3 4 5 6 7 8 9
Challenge	2 4 6 8 1 3 5 7 9
Soulution	2 4 6 8 1 3 5 7 9

It is interesting to note that the soulution to each achievement challenge is the number 9; in other words, if you use your achievement number as your personal number and refer to the chart above, the soulution given is always 9. This is because, regardless of which achievement number you have, you always need to overcome the fears associated with that aspect of your self we call ego.

The number 9 also has a special attribute when it appears as a person's achievement number. As the chart above shows, every other achievement number has a separate challenge and soulution. The 9 achievement number, however, has the same challenge and soulution; this is additional grace that counters its intensity. The 9 is the most intense of all the achievement numbers (ANs) because it also incorporates the challenges of the previous eight achievement numbers. When, however, a person with a 9 AN recognizes something is not working and does the opposite, it will work better. For example, a person with a 9 AN with control issues will become upset when others (2) ignore his advice. Or, a codependent person with a 9 AN will sacrifice herself for others (2). The soulution for both is to let go of

40   Finding Soulutions to Achievement Number Challenges

```
1 2 3 4 5 6 7 8 9
A B C D E F G H I
J K L M N O P Q R
S T U V W X Y Z
```

emotional and sentimental attachments (positive 2), compromise, and start doing what they love (9).

Brief Descriptions of the Challenge and Soulution Numbers

The **bold** words are negative interpretations; the plain-text words are positive interpretations.

1. **Ego too strong or too weak**
   Self-aware/innovator/paradigm buster

2. **Uncooperative/timid/sensitivity issues**
   Teamwork/good voice/intuitive

3. **Scattered/insecure/feels inadequate**
   Focus/mastery/visionary

4. **Lazy/judgmental/controlling**
   Organized/accepting/architect

5. **Rigid/impulsive/excessive**
   Flexibility/moderation/balance

6. **Perfectionist/irresponsible/martyr**
   Be of service/mentor/counselor

7. **Insecure/fearful/impatient/overly analytical**
   Patience/faith/trust/healer/teacher

8. **Anger/rebellious/bully/money issues**
   Organized/leader/delegates/wisdom

9. **Emotional/selfish/codependent/ controlling**
   Selfless/compassionate/universalistic

4

Determining Name Challenges

The formulas given in this chapter will enable you to identify a person's basic behavior patterns in any setting—professionally, socially, with family, and in relationships—in less than sixty seconds, knowing only his or her name!

Each part of an individual's name pertains to different aspects of life.

The *first name* provides the basis for an instant analysis of general challenges faced by an individual or a business in their workday behavior patterns.

An individual's *middle name* reveals information that will aid the understanding of emotional patterns.

The *surname,* or last name, (the person's name at birth, not a married name) can be used to understand birth family characteristics and dynamics. (However, in the case of adoption, the adopted surname should be used.)

Two different methods are presented in this chapter. The first is known as the 1st Vowel/1st Consonant Challenge, or V/CC, and the second is an interpretation of the numeric equivalent of all the letters of a given name.

1ST VOWEL/1ST CONSONANT CHALLENGE
OR V/CC FORMULA DERIVATION

Whether for first, middle, or surname, the basic V/CC formula is the same. It is derived in the following way:

1. First use the letter-to-number conversion chart to determine the numeric equivalent of the first vowel and the first consonant of the name. (Remember that the bolded letters in the chart indicate the "vowels.")

   Example A: A r thur—The first vowel is *A* (= 1); the first consonant is *R* (= 9)

   Example B: D e borah—The first consonant is *D* (= 4); the first vowel is *E* (= 5)

1	2	3	4	5	6	7	8	9
A	B	C	D	**E**	F	G	H	**I**
J	K	L	M	N	**O**	P	Q	R
S	T	U	V	**W**	X	**Y**	Z	

2. Add the numeric equivalent of the first vowel and that of the first consonant together. Then reduce any double-digit numbers in the same way as for the achievement number determination. Write the result as the first part of the formula, preceding a slash mark.

   Example A: A r thur—*A*(1) + *R*(9) = 10; then reduce the 10 to 1 (1 + 0 = 1); write as 1/

   Example B: D e borah—*D*(4) + *E*(5) = 9; write as 9/

```
1 2 3 4 5 6 7 8 9
A B C D E F G H I
J K L M N O P Q R
S T U V W X Y Z
```
Determining Name Challenges   **43**

3. Next, subtract the smaller number from the larger number. (Whether you subtract the vowel number from the consonant number or vice versa, *the key is to subtract the smaller number from the larger number.*) Write the result as the second part of the formula following the slash mark.

> Example A: A r thur—$R(9) - A(1) = 8$; combined with the first total, it is written as 1/8
>
> Example B: D e borah—$E(5) - D(4) = 1$; combined with the first total, it is written as 9/1

When you are performing the computation, you may encounter one or more of the following situations, which require special treatment.

Multiple consonants. If two or more consonants combine to form a single sound (*Br*ian, *Ch*arlene, *Fr*ank, *Gl*enda, *Chr*istopher) add all the letters as one, then continue building the formula as usual. Using the first name of Christopher as an example:

- Add the numeric equivalent of the initial triple consonants, C ($= 3$) + H ($= 8$) + R ($= 9$), for a total of 20, and then reduce the 20 to 2 by adding $2 + 0$, which equals 2.
- Next, find the numeric equivalent of the first vowel, I, which is 9.
- Add the consonant total of 2 to the vowel total of 9 for a sum of 11. Reduce the 11 by adding $1+1 = 2$. Write the answer as 2/.
- Next, subtract the smaller number from the larger number. In this instance, subtract the consonant total of 2 from the vowel total of 9 for a result of 7.
- Write the final equation as 2/7.

Multiple vowels. Double vowels (*Aa*ron, *Ai*leen, Br*oo*k, C*ou*rtney, D*ai*sy) and triple vowels (L*oue*lla, L*oui*s, L*oui*se, L*owe*ll) are treated in the same way as double or triple consonants. However, the determination of vowel

```
1 2 3 4 5 6 7 8 9
A B C D E F G H I
J K L M N O P Q R
S T U V W X Y Z
```

44   Determining Name Challenges

combinations can be tricky, as it depends on how the name is pronounced. Use your ear to listen for the sound break. For example, a person named Louella may pronounce her name as "Louel la" or "Lou ella." The pronunciation of a name is very important because it determines which vowels to combine to form the V/CC; they in turn influence the resulting formula.

- In "*Louel* la" the first vowels would be O (= 6) + U (= 3) + E (= 5), which would total 14, which is reduced to a total of 5 (1 + 4 = 5). The numeric equivalent of the first consonant, L, is 3. The consonant total of 3 added to the vowel total of 5 results in the sum 8. The first part of the V/CC formula thus would be written as 8/.
- In "*Lou* ella" the first vowels would be O (= 6) + U (= 3), which would result in a total of 9. The consonant total of 3 (for L) added to the vowel total of 9 results in the sum 12, which is reduced to a total of 3 (1 + 2 = 3). The first part of the V/CC formula thus would be written as 3/.

Working with Zero. When subtracting two numbers, if the result is a zero (0), change the 0 to a 9; thus, 1 – 1 = 0 (or 2 – 2 = 0, and so on) becomes 9.

Rules for Figuring 1st Vowel/1st Consonant Challenge

- Always add prior to subtracting.
- The number derived by addition is always placed in front of the slash mark (X/), and the number derived via subtraction follows the slash mark (/X).
- Always subtract the smaller number from the larger number. (Use standard subtraction rules.)
- The formula is derived in the same way for any name of a person (first, middle, surname, or nickname), as well as for the name of a company or other organization, or a country, and so on.

```
1 2 3 4 5 6 7 8 9
A B C D E F G H I
J K L M N O P Q R
S T U V W X Y Z
```
Determining Name Challenges   **45**

Practice Deriving the V/CC Formula

Before taking the next step of using the V/CC formula to better understand behavior, practice deriving the equations for a few names, using the
letter-to-number conversion chart. Use the names of people you know
well so that when you go to the next step of interpretation you will be able
to verify the accuracy of the formulas and interpretations.

FIRST Name	ADD	SUBTRACT	RESULT
	Vowel + Consonant	Vowel − Consonant	
		(or smaller from larger number)	

MIDDLE Name	ADD	SUBTRACT	RESULT
	Vowel + Consonant	Vowel − Consonant	

LAST Name	ADD	SUBTRACT	RESULT
	Vowel + Consonant	Vowel − Consonant	

Interpretation Notes:

FIRST Name	ADD	SUBTRACT	RESULT
	Vowel + Consonant	Vowel − Consonant	

MIDDLE Name	ADD	SUBTRACT	RESULT
	Vowel + Consonant	Vowel − Consonant	

	1	2	3	4	5	6	7	8	9
	A	B	C	D	E	F	G	H	I
	J	K	L	M	N	O	P	Q	R
	S	T	U	V	W	X	Y	Z	

46   Determining Name Challenges

LAST Name	ADD	SUBTRACT	RESULT
	Vowel + Consonant	Vowel − Consonant	

Interpretation Notes:

FIRST Name	ADD	SUBTRACT	RESULT
	Vowel + Consonant	Vowel − Consonant	

MIDDLE Name	ADD	SUBTRACT	RESULT
	Vowel + Consonant	Vowel − Consonant	

LAST Name	ADD	SUBTRACT	RESULT
	Vowel + Consonant	Vowel − Consonant	

Interpretation Notes:

INTERPRETING V/CC FORMULAS

As we have seen, each aspect of our given name indicates particular aspects of our life. Thus the V/CC formula reveals specific challenges for each aspect of a person's name.

Our first name represents how we behave in our everyday life, our "work world," as well as our attempts to balance our working

environment with our spiritual growth. It also identifies possible
health issues that may arise due to the stress of dealing with our
challenges.

Our middle name reflects the way we feel and behave in our personal relationships. A middle name reveals the type of people we
are attracted to and why we are attracted to them. If there is no
middle name, such people have chosen to learn to balance their
emotions in this lifetime; they can either be very emotionally
intense or flat.

Our last names offer clues as to why we picked our birth or adoptive
families.

These specifics should be kept in mind as you interpret the V/CC
formula for each name, using the basic number concepts and their
positive and negative attributes. I cannot stress enough the importance
of possessing a familiarity with these basic concepts and the positive
and negative characteristics of the numbers 1 through 9 (given in the
Table of Positive and Negative Attributes of Numbers, in chapter 1,
pages 13–15).

The number to the right in the V/CC formula indicates the basic
issues involved, as outlined in the *Table of Basic Number Concepts,*
reproduced below from chapter 1:

TABLE OF BASIC NUMBER CONCEPTS

1 = Issues of the Ego Self

2 = Issues Involving Others

3 = Issues Involving Communication, Social Interactions,
Feelings of Inadequacy

4 = Issues Involving Details and "Getting Things Done"

5 = Issues Involving Change and Movement

6 = Issues Involving Family, Community, Relationships, Responsibility

7 = Issues Involving Abandonment, Trust, Skepticism, and Control

8 = Issues Involving Power, Money, Control, and Status

9 = Issues Involving Selflessness

0 = Issues Related to Spirit

The basic issue revealed by the right-hand number overlays the factors indicated by the left-hand number in the V/CC equation. For example: a 2/1 combination indicates that issues of the ego self (1) can make interacting with others (2) challenging. Keep in mind that these combinations represent the blueprint an individual used to begin life. As a challenge is resolved, it can be transmuted into a strength.

When you want to interpret the V/CC formula for a name, work from right to left. For example, we computed the V/CC for the name Christopher as 2/7. Starting with the basic issues for number 7 (that is, abandonment, trust, skepticism, and control), elaborating them with the positive and negative attributes of numbers, we can decipher that his V/CC indicates that in the workplace he may be overly analytical and worry that others may not meet his high standards, so he will overcommit himself because of a need to gain acceptance and avoid embarrassment. In relationships, he will find it easier to do for others than allow others to do for him. He has a need for control due to his vulnerability issues.

Practice V/CC Interpretation

1. For each name whose V/CC formula you calculated above, identify the basic issue (revealed by the right-hand number) and elaborate your understanding of its influence on the issues indicated by the left-hand number. Fill in the Interpretation Notes. Remember that the arena of life varies by whether you are interpreting the first, middle, or last name challenges.

2. Next, refer to the descriptions given in the *Table of Predefined 1st Vowel/1st Consonant Challenges (V/CC)*, Appendix I. Compare the two results. You'll be surprised at how accurately they match.

Repeated practice is what will enable you to identify behavior patterns in sixty seconds or less.

Interpreting Special Challenge Numbers

As you compute the V/CC formula for a name, pay particular attention if any of the karmic numbers (13, 14, 16, or 19) appear as the result of adding two numbers. Even though the double-digit number is reduced to obtain the final formula, the fact that a karmic number is involved adds spice to the recipe. The interpretations you should keep in mind are detailed below. For example, the consonant *M* in Michael added to the vowel *I* equals 13, which is reduced to 4. The subsurface 13 has a definite influence on the 4, so the negative interpretation for both numbers should be studied. These hidden karmic numbers play a subtle but noticeable role in the final determination of a behavior pattern.

Karmic Number Interpretations

13 • A feeling of insecurity, inadequacy, or inferiority can lead to low self-esteem, hindering the ability to let go and allow change to take place. It also indicates difficulty in accepting advice from others and the possibility of procrastination.

14 • A tendency toward excess (too much/too little). Some stubbornness. A desire for control. Hastiness can lead to accidents and long periods of recovery.

16 • Displays a lack of "faith." A fear of looking foolish if things don't go well can lead to making up rules to match the situation. Main fear is being rejected (abandoned).

19 • Difficulty balancing male/female energy; can swing between the compassion of Mother Teresa and the ruthlessness of Genghis Kahn. Can have major self-esteem issues. Always indicates some form of distress or suffering (emotional, mental, or physical).

Example: H e rbert—H (8) + E (5) = 13, which is reduced to 4 (1 + 3 = 4); then 8 − 5 = 3; the result is 4/3. (The result can also be written as 13//4/3 to indicate the hidden influence of 13.) For interpretation purposes, use the 4/3, keeping the 13 interpretation in the back of your mind, aware that it is a challenge number that carries special energy.

V/CCS FOR COUNTRIES

Use your general knowledge of a country to determine the accuracy of its V/CC. The thumbnail descriptions of the countries' behavior patterns are generally reflected in political actions, words, and deeds. Remember that when two numbers are subtracted from each other and the remainder is 0, it should be changed to a 9 (e.g., Ireland: I [9] + R [9] = 18, which is reduced to 9 [1 + 8 = 9]; 9 − 9 = 0, which is changed to 9, resulting in 9/9).

United States (United Kingdom, United Arab Emirates)
U (3) + N (5) = 8   5 − 3 = 2   Result = <u>8/2</u>

This country generally wants other countries to know what it wants without having to explain it to them. It can be imperial. The U as the first letter brings with it both creativity and frustration if desires are ignored.

Canada
C (3) + A (1) = 4   3 − 1 = 2   Result = <u>4/2</u>

This country likes cleanliness, order, system, and structure. It does not like being forced to make changes, either internally or externally. Its citizens have very strong individual belief systems. At times this country finds other countries to be inconsistent and unreliable. The A as the last letter indicates there can be regrets about the results of totally relying on logic and ignoring intuitive feelings.

Mexico
M (4) + E (5) = 9   5 − 4 = 1   Result = <u>9/1</u>

This country needs to be thanked, recognized, or appreciated for

```
1 2 3 4 5 6 7 8 9
A B C D E F G H I
J K L M N O P Q R
S T U V W X Y Z
```
Determining Name Challenges   **51**

whatever it does or it may ignore the needs of others and only do for itself. Its citizens may have to go through pain and suffering to learn to open their hearts.

Brazil

B (2) + R (9) = 11, reduced (1 + 1) = 2 + A (1) = 3   2 – 1 = 1
Result = 3/1

A lack of confidence could make the citizens of this country overly amiable. Culturally, they like to "window shop" (i.e., look at pretty things, whether people or objects, but not necessarily buy). The B can make them sensitive; the R can make them emotionally intense. The Z can bring frustration and accompanying emotions when things don't go the way they expect. The frustration may come from the combination of the BR, which equals 11. An 11 allows a country to see the way things ought to be but not to have the power or the opportunity to make them that way.

Venezuela

V (4) + E (5) = 9   5 – 4 = 1   Result = 9/1

This country wants recognition for planning abilities and organizational skills; it can be egocentric and stubborn. It has a tendency to poke its nose into other countries' business. There are definite control issues and a need to be recognized for "good" deeds (9). The A as the last letter indicates there can be regrets about the results of totally relying on logic and ignoring intuitive feelings.

Great Britain

This one is a little tricky—there's a double consonant blend (GR) as well as a double vowel blend (EA). The double consonant sum of 16, a karmic number, should be considered as an influence. G (7) + R (9) = 16, reduced (1 + 6) = 7; E (5) + A (1) = 6; add the consonant total to the vowel total 7 + 6 = 13/4 (note the influence of the 13, a karmic number); and 7 – 6 = 1; Result = 4/1

The subsurface 16 (*GR*) brings a messianic energy to "save people from themselves" as well as a need to be validated for making the world a better place. The 16 can also indicate a tendency toward self-righteousness. The negative subsurface 13 can indicate feelings of inadequacy and a tendency to be skeptical of the intentions or ideas of others, leading to reactionary behavior patterns. The V/CC of 4/1, applied to this country, may be interpreted in several ways: a lack of confidence leading to a need to be in control; a national identity directly linked to what they "do," not who they are; or too much reliance on data, facts, and logic and not enough use of an innate intuitiveness.

Ireland

I (9) + *R* (9) = 18, reduced   1 + 8 = 9   9 − 9 = 0, which is changed to 9   Result 9/9

The double nines bring constant agitation and intensity. This country has difficulty letting go and moving on. Within the 18, the 8 indicates violence over individual rights or subjugation (1) involving foreigners (9).

France

F (6) + *R* (9) = 15, reduced (1 + 5) = 6 + *A* (1) = 7   6 − 1 = 5
Result = 7/5

This country is apprehensive about making changes (5) because it does not want to be embarrassed or humiliated (7).

Estonia

E (5) + *S* (1) = 6   5 − 1 = 4   Result = 6/4

E as the first letter can make this country emotional and impulsive. It wants to be responsible for itself (6). It could be somewhat unrealistic in its expectations for itself or of others (6). If it is given responsibility, it wants things done in a practical/logical way (4). The *A* as the last letter can indicate a tendency to think too much prior to taking action based on past miscalculations. The 6/4 also indicates a desire to control others (4) by telling them what is best for them (6), but not wanting to be bothered by the details (4) of how to resolve things (6). The *A* as the last letter indicates there can be regrets about the results of totally relying on logic and ignoring intuitive feelings.

Russia

R (9) + *U* (3) = 12, reduced (1 + 2) = 3   9 − 3 = 6   Result = 3/6

The *R* can make this country very intense. The *U* reveals underlying frustration. The *SS* is seldom satisfied, which can lead to more *I* intensity. The *A* as the last letter indicates hindsight is better than foresight. The 3/6 indicates that it scatters its energy by taking on too many responsibilities and can be unforgiving of self or others because of high expectations or perfectionist tendencies. The *A* as the last letter indicates there can be regrets about the results of totally relying on logic and ignoring intuitive feelings.

China

C (3) + *H* (8) = 11, reduced (1 + 1) = 2 + *I* (9) = 11, reduced (1 + 1) = 2
9 − 2 = 7;   Result = 2/7

The *CH* equals 11 and indicates this country can be zealous in its belief systems. The 2/7 country can be very impatient (7) with others (2)—they see it, why can't/don't others? Individuals in this culture may not speak up because of timidity or a hypersensitivity to the feelings of others. They are concerned about being "wrong" or misperceived by others, and as a result being humiliated, embarrassed, or ostracized. The *A* as the last letter indicates there can be regrets about the results of totally relying on logic and ignoring intuitive feelings.

COMBINING INSIGHTS FROM
ACHIEVEMENT NUMBERS AND NAMES

When performing V/CC interpretations, it is important to always keep the achievement number (AN) in mind (the methodology for computing an achievement number is given in chapter 2). The achievement number is the nucleus of the personality. The combination of the 1st vowel/1st consonant challenge in conjunction with the achievement number enables you to zero in on specific patterns and increase the accuracy of your analysis.

Combining First Name V/CCs and Achievement Numbers

As the first name is related to work environment behavior, the combined insights of the first name V/CC and the AN are applied to that context.

Example: *Abraham, April 30*
Abraham's V/CC is 3/1 and his AN is 34/7.

With a V/CC of 3/1, Abraham doesn't always finish what he starts because he doesn't want to be judged by others (3). Also feelings of insecurity can affect his self-esteem (1). Combined with his 34/7 AN, he can have abandonment anxieties, which make him fearful of making mistakes (7). The 4 of the 34, combined with the anxieties of the 7 and 1 can make him overly logical and a bit of a reactionary. A person with a V/CC of 3/1 can be a "window shopper" who enjoys looking at pretty things, human or merchandise, but doesn't always buy.

Example: *Cynthia, November 20*
Cynthia's V/CC is 1/4 and her AN is 31/4.

Cynthia's low self-esteem (1) can lead to stubbornness or procrastination. She may want to "go by the book" (4). A V/CC of 1/4, combined with a 4 AN, indicates she may be too logical, a bit of a reactionary, and have a need to be in charge. This would tie in to her need for control (4) due to low levels of self-confidence (1). The 31 of her AN again emphasizes feelings of inadequacy (3) and low self-esteem (1). With the last letter of her first name being *A,* it's a pretty safe bet to say Cynthia does not sufficiently trust her intuition.

Example: *Julie, November 12*

Julie's V/CC is 4/2 and her AN is 23/5.

Her V/CC indicates that Julie finds people to be inconsistent and therefore has a tendency to put her energy into her work. She likes to maintain order, system, and structure. Her V/CC of 4/2 combined with an AN of 5 indicates she could be a little rigid when dealing with others. The 23 in her AN indicates feelings of inadequacy (3) and a sensitivity to the opinions of others (2); even though she wants her freedom of choice, she is apprehensive about going for it.

Example: *Michael, February 28*

Michael's V/CC is 4/5 and his AN is 30/3.

His V/CC indicates that unless Michael can determine what will occur and when (5), he becomes overly cautious and a little stubborn about making changes (4). Combine this with the 3 AN, and we can see that this pattern is the result of feelings of insecurity or inadequacy. The 4 of the 4/5 V/CC is actually a 13. This indicates that feelings of inadequacy (3) and low self-esteem (1) are the catalyst for the resistance to change.

Example: *Sheila, December 26*

Sheila's V/CC is 5/4 and her AN is 38/2.

Sheila's V/CC indicates that she does not like change unless she is the change agent, and then changes cannot come soon enough (this is shown by the 14, from *E* + *I*, underlying the 5 of her V/CC). Her V/CC of 5/4 combined with a 2 AN indicates that she doesn't like change because it will force her to speak up and she doesn't want to hurt the feelings of others. She also has difficulty letting go of emotional and sentimental attachments (2) and avoids self-empowerment (8) because of feelings of inadequacy (3).

Example: *Steven, May 19*

Steven's V/CC is 8/2 and his AN is 24/6.

1	2	3	4	5	6	7	8	9
A	B	C	D	E	F	G	H	I
J	K	L	M	N	O	P	Q	R
S	T	U	V	W	X	Y	Z	

56   Determining Name Challenges

Steven's V/CC of 8/2 indicates that he expects people to know what he wants without having to communicate his desires. His V/CC of 8/2 combined with an AN of 24/6 indicate that he can "suffer in silence" (2) as he burdens himself with the responsibilities of others. The S can indicate "seldom satisfied"; seldom being satisfied, for whatever reason, always brings stress. The 24 can indicate a need to be in control (4) of others (2) for their own best good (6).

Combining Middle Name V/CCs and Achievement Numbers

Insights gained from looking at the middle name V/CC and achievement number of a person are particularly pertinent to the arena of relationships.

Example: *Ann, September 16*
Middle name V/CC of 2/9 and a 25/7 AN.

With a middle name V/CC of 2/9, she can be overly sensitive to the needs of others with codependent behavior patterns. She can immerse herself in doing for others, until she reaches her saturation point of being "good." At this point, she needs to totally withdraw (25/7 AN) and take time to recenter herself. She needs to be loved, recognized, and appreciated emotionally; otherwise she may withdraw or become depressed (7). She has a need to be needed as well as a need to be in control (both 7 issues.) The 5 can make her apprehensive about letting go and moving on (5) because of a need for another (2).

Example: *Elizabeth, August 5*
Middle name V/CC of 8/2 and a 13/4 AN.

The V/CC of 8/2 indicates this person can be a bit imperial (expecting others to automatically know what she wants). Combined with a 13/4 AN, she can be controlling and stubborn (4), caused by underlying feelings of inadequacy (3) and low self-esteem (1). She may remain in a relationship long after she should have left it (13/4). The single-digit total for Elizabeth is 7; emotionally, sevens have a hard time first opening up, and once they do, they have a hard time letting go.

Example: *Jay, May 21*
Middle name V/CC of 9/7 and a 26/8 AN.

With a middle name V/CC of 9/7, this person can voluntarily become an emotional pincushion for others. He can be withdrawn emotionally and need reinforcement that he is loved. He can also be disconnected emotionally (9 and 7). Combined with his 26/8 AN, there is an indication he may be afraid to be himself in a relationship and may find it easier to assume a role than to be assertive. Or, he may be very controlling (8), fearful of being abandoned (7).

Example: *Marie, July 29*
Middle name V/CC of 5/3 and a 36/9 AN.

With a middle name V/CC of 5/3, this person does not like change and can make it unpleasant for those who try to force change on her. This V/CC combined with her 36/9 AN indicates she can take on the role of "cosmic mother" (6) and has difficulty expressing her heartfelt truths. It's much easier for her to give than receive (9). Can be in codependent relationships as the dominant partner. Can be sarcastic.

Example: *Richard, January 6*
Middle name V/CC of 9/9 and a 7 AN.

This person can go either of two ways; he may be full of compassion and understanding (9), or he may emotionally isolate himself because of vulnerability issues (9). He can isolate himself from others by being nasty, intense, controlling, depressed, overly dramatic in his responses, or angry (all negative 9 behaviors). This V/CC combined with his 7 AN indicates he may find it easier to give than receive or be emotionally closed off (7). His abandonment issues make him more of an observer than a participant in his relationships.

Example: *Susan, September 11*

Middle name V/CC of 4/2 and a 20/2 AN.

With a middle name V/CC of 4/2, she finds people inconsistent and will get involved with people who are emotionally weaker because of control/codependency issues associated with her 2 AN. Her 4/2 V/CC combined with her 20/2 AN indicate there is a definite trend toward "broken-wing" relationships. She is the *fixer* in the relationship but becomes disappointed when her partner does not acknowledge her contributions. The *S* indicates she is seldom satisfied (wanting to make things better), and the *U* indicates underlying frustration caused by not expressing her dissatisfaction.

Combining Last Name V/CCs and Achievement Numbers

The V/CC of an individual's birth or adoptive family's surname reveals family dynamics. The energy of the V/CC is a reflection of the way the "male" energy behaves (could be mother or father, whoever is dominant in the household). Just as with the first and middle name V/CCs, you will want to combine the insights of the last name V/CC with an understanding of the influence of the individual's achievement number. However, here, to avoid using any real last names, I will only analyze the V/CC.

Example: *An—6/4*

The dominant energy in this family is the tendency to give advice but not be bothered by the details of how to achieve resolution. It can also include perfectionist tendencies and the need to be in control.

Example: *Bu—5/1*

The dominant energy in this family can be expressed in two different ways, depending on how the dominant person feels in a given situation: either inflexible and resistant to change (5) if the person is not in charge (1), or overly amenable (5) if the person is but is feeling insecure (1).

Example: *Cli—6/3*

The dominant energy in this family can be unforgiving or even sarcastic (3) toward those who don't seem to appreciate the advice being given (6). It can also have perfectionist tendencies (6) related to feelings of insecurity and inadequacy (3).

Example: *De—9/1*

The dominant energy in this family can be expressed as the tendency to tie personal identity to doing for others (9) due to low self-esteem (1) or the tendency to be controlling in an effort to make things go "their way." The opposite is also true; it can be expressed as the tendency to act only on behalf of self without regard for others.

Example: *Du—7/1*

The dominant energy in this family can be expressed as the tendency to find it easier to give than receive due to issues of vulnerability and abandonment, along with a tendency to give advice even if it wasn't sought. The dominant parent may withdraw at times of stress.

Example: *Ma—5/3*

The dominant energy in this family resists change (5) because of feelings of inadequacy and uncertainty (3). The *M* (a 4) indicates that the dominant person can be stubborn or manipulative because of the conviction that he or she has already figured it out *(A)*. The stubbornness can also be related to uncertainty or feelings of inadequacy.

Example: *Schu—6/9*

The dominant energy in this family results in high expectations for family members (6), which can lead to conflict and unhappiness for all parties. It can also mean that the individual becomes an impractical social reformer (9) who spreads his or her energy too thin trying to do too much, for too many, with too little resources, and then gets caught up in self-blame.

DERIVING AND INTERPRETING THE NUMBERS OF FULL NAMES

In addition to the V/CC formula, the numeric energy of every letter in a name can be added together to provide additional insights about an individual. Names of businesses or corporations, groups, countries, or pets as well as people can be analyzed. Add the numeric equivalent of each letter and reduce as necessary. Write the result in the same way as the achievement number is written: with the double-digit sum to the left of the slash mark and the reduced number to the right. The numbers are then interpreted using the following lists of attributes. The single-digit total provides the basis for the fundamental interpretation; however, if you want to look a little deeper, look at the attributes for the numbers of the double-digit sum as well.

First Name Attributes

Converting the letters of a first name into their numeric equivalents reveals the type of work environment the person prefers as well as public personality traits.

1 • Likes to be the initiator, the leader. May like to work alone. Can be a "Yes" person. Can be a "No!" person.

2 • Seeks cooperation, partnership, mediation. Can be a team player.

3 • Needs harmonious and pleasant working environment (visual as well as physical). Not very confrontational. Can be scattered. Can be very sociable. Can have a sense of the rhythm of life. Loves music. Needs assignments that call for creative solutions. Does not care for paperwork. Work area needs to be physically pleasant (pastel colors and personal objects in the environment).

4 • Wants order, system, and structure. May "go by the book." May get lost in minutiae. Is logical and may want to be the "boss." Can be somewhat stubborn and a tad confrontational. Can be an excellent "worker bee." Is a natural architect.

5 • Needs constant change or gets bored. Learns best by *doing,* not by *reading*—a "hands-on" person. May only be concerned with concepts and not pay attention to details. Does not like any kind of paperwork.

6 • Likes to serve, counsel, and advise in any capacity. Can be a perfectionist. May take on too much responsibility or want to advise but not assume responsibility. A confidant for others.

7 • Very analytical and intense. Can be highly intuitive. Likes to solve problems. Likes to work alone. Is not very social. May feel a need to do for others. Can be passive-aggressive toward authority if suggestions are rejected. Authority figures must *earn* this person's respect. Concerned about making mistakes and how they might reflect on personal integrity. Impatient. Good with figures. Wants to share knowledge. Enjoys learning, teaching, instructing, or analyzing.

8 • Likes to initiate, orchestrate, and delegate. Can be very logical. Wants to manage. Can be dictatorial. Has a natural sense for the form, fit, and function of things. May become frustrated if "abilities" are not recognized. Likes being *responsible* for organizing, orchestrating, and completing big projects. Can be a manager or a natural leader. Business oriented. Can *"make it happen!"*

9 • Can easily get along with everyone or no one at all. Loves (or is attracted to) the drama and emotional intensity of daily living. Can be an actor/actress. Enjoys long-distance travel. Can be compassionate and selfless in service to others or very egocentric. May become overburdened by accepting or seeking more responsibility than he or she can comfortably handle. Would make an excellent healer. May have a natural affinity for the electrical or electronic.

1	2	3	4	5	6	7	8	9
A	B	C	D	E	F	G	H	I
J	K	L	M	N	O	P	Q	R
S	T	U	V	W	X	Y	Z	

62   Determining Name Challenges

Convert and Interpret First Names and Nicknames

Use the letter-to-number conversion chart to convert several first names, then interpret them using the first name attributes given above. If a person goes by a nickname, try doing the numbers to see if her nickname matches how her behavior differs from the behavior her birth name would indicate.

Example: A first name of Samuel

S A M U E L

$1 + 1 + 4 + 3 + 5 + 3 = 17$ $1 + 7 = 8$ $\underline{17/8}$

If the first name is Samuel, the name total is 8; if you want to look a little deeper, look at the attributes for the 1 and 7 as well.

A first name of _____

corresponding numbers: = _____

A first name of _____

= _____

A first name of _____

= _____

A first name of _____

= _____

A nickname of _____

= _____

A nickname of _____

= _____

Middle Name Attributes

Our middle name represents how we behave emotionally, the type of people we are attracted to, and why we are attracted to them. The information presented here is a fraction of what is taken into consideration when determining someone's emotional personality; however, as a thumbnail sketch of basic behavior patterns, the attributes given below are accurate. People with middle names that reduce to 1, 2, 6, 7, or 9 may have codependency issues. If there is no middle name, that individual has chosen this lifetime to balance his or her emotions, with a starting point of being either very emotionally inhibited or emotionally intense. If there are multiple middle names, combine them to form one name for purposes of analysis.

If the individual chooses to be known by his middle name,* he will experience emotional situations in his everyday (work world) life that could bring frustrations. It has been my experience that when a person changes back to his first name for everyday use, rather than using his middle name, his life usually changes for the better within three weeks!

1 • Wants to be in charge or may feel unworthy. May feel emotionally self-sufficient. May be attracted to strong-willed (or weak-willed) people as a counterbalance.

2 • Needs a partner; has a strong need to share. May be attracted to codependent relationships. Desires harmony and peace; to keep it, may not always speak up in a timely manner. May be a compromiser.

3 • Can be a cheerleader/optimist, sometimes to an extreme. Not very confrontational; dislikes disharmony. A romantic. Could be moody and have emotional "ups and downs." May have feelings of emotional insecurity. Can be unforgiving.

4 • Wants emotional stability. Can be somewhat judgmental. May procrastinate until certain of emotions. Finds it easier to give than receive. Can be controlling and emotionally stubborn. May not be very romantic.

---

*This is true even if it was the parents' intent that the child be known by his middle name.

5 • Can be either too rigid or too flexible. May be flirtatious. Emotionally flighty. Relationships meet physical needs. May seek multiple relationships.

6 • Wants to be the cosmic mother/father. Domesticity is very important. Loves love. Likes to counsel others (whether others want it or not). Faithful and true. High expectations for self and others can make relationships difficult. Can be a perfectionist. May be attracted to codependent relationships as the caregiver.

7 • Somewhat aloof and withdrawn. Needs a spiritual partner. Can be controlling to "make certain" everything goes well. Has a very strong need to be needed. Feels hurt when advice is not accepted. Finds it easy to give but hard to receive; has difficulty being emotionally vulnerable.

8 • Has a temper. Wants to be the boss. Wants to delegate to others. Can become frustrated if partner does not share intensity. Everything must pay. Usually not romantic.

9 • Can be loving, spiritual, unselfish, and compassionate or very emotional, intense, and egocentric. Finds it difficult to "let go" emotionally; has a tendency to "hold" emotions for others. Could be a "Mother Theresa." May have the self-perception of being a "great lover," either physically or spiritually.

Convert and Interpret Middle Names

Use the letter-to-number conversion chart to convert several middle names, then interpret them using the middle name attributes given above.

Example: A middle name of Benjamin

B E N J A M I N

2 + 5 + 5 + 1 + 1 + 4 + 9 + 5 = 32   3 + 2 = 5   32/5

If the middle name is Benjamin, the name total is 5. However, if you want to look a little deeper, look at the attributes for the 2 and 3 as well.

A middle name of _____

corresponding numbers: = _____

A middle name of _____

                                                          = _____

A middle name of _____

                                                          = _____

A middle name of _____

                                                          = _____

A middle name of _____

                                                          = _____

Last Name Attributes

The single-digit total of the numeric equivalents of the letters of a person's last name reveals family dynamics when it is compared with the individual's achievement number. This comparison also reveals what each person in the family is to learn from the family and what the family is to learn from that person.

Do you want to know why you chose your family? To find out, add all of the letters of your last name together and reduce to a single digit. Use either your surname at birth or, if you were adopted, use your adoptive family's surname. Look at the negative characteristics of that number and then compare it with the negative characteristics of your single-digit achievement number. That's where the answer lies.

For example: my last name, Brill, reduces to an 8 and my AN is 3. With an achievement number of 3, I was a bit of a butterfly, never settling on anything for too long. The reason I picked this family was to learn to be better organized, to get things done, and to set an example by "walking my talk."

5

The Planes of Expression

Another Level of Understanding

Another level of interpretation of behavior is made possible by the use of a chart known as the *Table of Personality Characteristics*. This table shows the distribution of the letters of the alphabet through four planes of expression, mental, physical, emotional, and intuitive; and three categories, inspired, dual, and balanced. When a person's name is compared with the chart, it can reveal his or her approach to life.

TABLE OF PERSONALITY CHARACTERISTICS

	Mental	Physical	Emotional	Intuitive
Inspired	A	E	O R I Z	K
Dual	H J N P	W	B S T X	F Q U Y
Balanced	G L	D M	- - - -	C V

The table is used by determining how many letters of a name appear in each of the planes of expression, and then referring to the interpretations related to the number of letters in a given plane (given below). In addition, the number of letters in the three categories on the left help to clarify whether an individual is a starter (inspired) or follower (balanced) or both (dual), depending on the situation and the person's level of confidence.

DEFINITIONS OF THE FOUR PLANES
OF EXPRESSION

Mental Plane: An emphasis on the mental plane indicates that logic, not imagination, rules decision making. A person with this emphasis can be very skeptical until facts are proven to his or her satisfaction. Such a person has a fine mind and can demonstrate brilliant thinking when placed in leadership positions. A person with this emphasis can also be strong willed, determined, and able to maintain a positive state of mind, and may sometimes be calculating. These traits appear in everyday life, such as at work and at home, and in relation to friendships as well as finances.

Physical Plane: A person with an emphasis on the physical plane also displays little imagination and is oriented toward the tangible things in life: common sense, practicality, health, physical activity, sports, and above all else, sex.

Emotional Plane: For a person with an emphasis on this plane, sentiment rather than logic rules; logic does not play a large role in his or her decision-making process or personal plans. Imagination, inspiration, vision, and creativity without much thought of practicality are the rule. A person with an emphasis on the emotional plane tries very hard to encourage warmth and beauty. He or she can be very sympathetic, but also wants sympathy in return.

Intuitive Plane: A person with an emphasis on this plane is guided by revelations and possesses significant inner knowledge, which surpasses facts and even imagination. A person with a majority of name letters in this column can be a true believer or a practitioner of universal love. Innovative and inventive personality traits are present.

68   The Planes of Expression

```
1 2 3 4 5 6 7 8 9
A B C D E F G H I
J K L M N O P Q R
S T U V W X Y Z
```

UNDERSTANDING THE THREE CATEGORIES

Inspired: A majority of name letters on this line indicates the ability and willingness to originate or start things.

Dual: Dual emphasis indicates strengths in originating and starting things paired with the ability to follow through on one's own ideas as well as those of others.

Balanced: A majority of letters in this category indicates a person who is good at completing whatever has been started. It also indicates that the person will always be hardworking on his or her plane of prominence (mental, physical, emotional, or intuitive). An emphasis here may also give others the impression that the individual is a "copycat" at times.

Using the Table of Personality Characteristics

Ideally, the complete name (first, middle, and last) as it appears on a birth certificate or court document should be used. (The court document is needed for a person who has legally changed his or her name, other than for marriage.) If all you have is a first name, then just use it, keeping in mind that the results will be pertinent primarily to the personality approach taken in the workplace and daily interactions. The middle name will provide insight into the person's emotional responses and relationships, and the last name identifies the family dynamic or energy. The negative interpretation could be what's holding you back. The positive interpretation can help you follow your passion and fulfill your destiny. The full name combines all these factors for a comprehensive assessment. This table can also be used for the names of businesses, governments, and countries.

Sample:

1. Put a tiny "tic" mark just above each letter of the name, as shown in the table below, which is marked as it would be for my complete name.

Person's Name: Michael Richard Brill

	Mental	Physical	Emotional	Intuitive	Totals
Inspired	A	E	O R I Z	K	9
Dual	H J N P	W	B S T X	F Q U Y	3
Balanced	G L	D M	- - - -	C V	7
Totals	7	3	7	2	

2. Add the number of marks vertically to show the plane emphasis. For my name, the results are: mental plane—7 letters, physical plane—3 letters, emotional plane—7 letters, and intuitive plane—2 letters.

3. Add the number of marks horizontally to determine the category emphasis. For my name, the results are: inspired—9 letters, dual—3 letters, and balanced—7 letters.

4. Consult the interpretations of personality characteristics below (pages 72–82), which are keyed to the number of letters in each plane (mental, physical, emotional, intuitive). The highest total indicates the primary behavior pattern. If two or more planes have the same total, those planes have equal influence.

5. Note the dominant expression and circle that on the form, as shown for my name:

Dominant Expression: (Mental) Physical (Emotional) Intuitive

6. Note which category (inspired, dual, or balanced) has the highest total of letters and circle that on the form, as shown for my name:

Dominant Approach: (Inspired) Dual Balanced

Practice Tables

Fill in the following practice tables in the same way. Start by practicing with your birth name (first, middle, last) as it appears on your birth certificate, but omit any references such as Jr., Sr., or I, II, and so on. Then repeat for family members or friends or anyone you wish.

1. Put a tiny "tic" mark just above each letter of the name.

2.   Add the number of marks vertically to show the plane emphasis.
3.   Add the number of marks horizontally to determine the category emphasis.
4.   Consult the interpretations of personality characteristics below (pages 72–82), which are keyed to the number of letters in each plane of expression (mental, physical, emotional, intuitive).
5.   Note the dominant expression and circle that on the form.
6.   Note which category (inspired, dual, or balanced) has the highest total of letters and circle that on the form.

Person's Name: _____

	Mental	Physical	Emotional	Intuitive	Totals
Inspired	A	E	O R I Z	K	
Dual	H J N P	W	B S T X	F Q U Y	
Balanced	G L	D M	- - - -	C V	
Totals					

Dominant Expression: Mental   Physical   Emotional   Intuitive
Dominant Approach: Inspired   Dual   Balanced

Person's Name: _____

	Mental	Physical	Emotional	Intuitive	Totals
Inspired	A	E	O R I Z	K	
Dual	H J N P	W	B S T X	F Q U Y	
Balanced	G L	D M	- - - -	C V	
Totals					

Dominant Expression: Mental   Physical   Emotional   Intuitive
Dominant Approach: Inspired   Dual   Balanced

Person's Name: _____

	Mental	**Physical**	**Emotional**	**Intuitive**	**Totals**
Inspired	A	E	O R I Z	K	
Dual	H J N P	W	B S T X	F Q U Y	
Balanced	G L	D M	- - - -	C V	
Totals					

Dominant Expression: Mental   Physical   Emotional   Intuitive

Dominant Approach: Inspired   Dual   Balanced

Notes Regarding Interpretations

- An equal number of letters may appear in multiple columns; this could represent either a balanced approach to life or that two or more areas are out of balance.
- A minimum of a single number is required for activation of any plane.
- Four or more letters in the emotional plane or the inspired category can indicate temperamental outbursts.
- On any of the planes of expression, 5 is not a particularly good number to have in a chart for education; it acts as a blocker to education and training because of a tendency of not focusing on the details or becoming bored.
- Ten or more letters under a single heading indicate this area is significantly out of balance. If this is the case, change the double-digit number into a single-digit number in the following way: 10 = 1, 11 = 2, 12 = 3, and so on, and then consult the interpretation for that number.

1	2	3	4	5	6	7	8	9
A	B	C	D	E	F	G	H	I
J	K	L	M	N	O	P	Q	R
S	T	U	V	W	X	Y	Z	

72   The Planes of Expression

INTERPRETATIONS OF PERSONALITY CHARACTERISTICS BASED ON THE PLANES OF EXPRESSION

After using the *Table of Personality Characteristics* to determine the areas of emphasis, refer to the following interpretations indicated by the number of letters in the given plane of expression.

Mental Plane Interpretations

1 Letter on the Mental Plane: Egocentric, tends to force own thoughts and ideas on others. Can be stubborn. Often makes decisions too late. Can be witty. On many occasions, too easily talked out of own ideas.

2 Letters on the Mental Plane: Needs the support and agreement of others when stating ideas or plans. Feels knowledgeable, but is afraid to meet opposition alone. Can be musically talented. Likes to collect things. Can become too involved with details.

3 Letters on the Mental Plane: Talks boastfully about self, interests, and plans. Has controversial ideas; usually not considered a practical person because of extreme imagination. Tends to exaggerate to overcome feelings of mental inferiority. Too high strung for long, hard physical labor.

4 Letters on the Mental Plane: Determined, but can become tied down by being too cautious. Is often held back by the tendency to be overly serious. Good planner, executive, and manager. Many life experiences will involve family and in-laws. Skeptical and stubborn at times. Envies those perceived as more successful.

5 Letters on the Mental Plane: Curious and nosy; lacking in mental discipline. Cannot stand monotony, resulting in frequent changes in opinions and difficulty in sticking with an activity unless good

1	2	3	4	5	6	7	8	9
A	B	C	D	E	F	G	H	I
J	K	L	M	N	O	P	Q	R
S	T	U	V	W	X	Y	Z	

The Planes of Expression **73**

at it. A natural promoter, can be successful in sales. Likes public service. Likes to study bizarre and unusual subjects.

6 Letters on the Mental Plane: Can be counted on to do what has been agreed to. Has a tendency to meddle in the affairs of others. Very sensitive to criticism. Often feels unappreciated, mainly because of assuming too many inappropriate responsibilities and feeling the burden. Life presents many emotional affairs, some of which may be unusual or unsought. Cares greatly for children and family. Education in the arts and sciences is beneficial.

7 Letters on the Mental Plane: Prefers to be alone and work alone. Finds it nearly impossible to spontaneously enjoy life; is analytical and very intense. Holds resentment too long when humiliated or embarrassed; this results in a further withdrawal to gather more data, so as to prevent a future reoccurrence. Can be quite chatty with familiar people or if well acquainted with the subject being discussed.

8 Letters on the Mental Plane: Very ambitious. A natural executive. Likes to receive recognition for accomplishments (seen as "big things") and can become disloyal if recognition is denied. Very materialistic. Finds making big money difficult; when money does come it is always needed for higher-than-expected expenses. Can appear well organized but often does not carry something through to completion.

9 Letters on the Mental Plane: Selfless in sharing ideas and giving assistance. Capable of interacting with people of all nationalities and races. Unconventional in thinking and habits, aloof, gullible. Mind tends to wander. Needs to be placed where personal concern about details is minimal.

0 Letters on the Mental Plane: Cannot reason confidently, lacks curiosity and inquisitiveness about life, and relies on unfeeling logic and cold facts.

Physical Plane Interpretations

1 Letter on the Physical Plane: Very active and enthusiastic. Not likely to finish what is started, as any plan, work, or activity quickly becomes tiresome. Impatient, dislikes delays. As sexual partner, does not put much emphasis on mate's preferences for pleasure. May get headaches. Can be restless. Very competitive. Procrastinates. Outgoing, original, and outstanding, especially if a total of 10 has been reduced to 1.

2 Letters on the Physical Plane: Can be very sensitive and empathetic toward others. Liable to lack self-confidence and want every detail in order prior to starting anything, including the sexual/sensual. Gets too involved in the minor details of dress, work, and so on. Holds on to useless or worn-out items for sentimental reasons. Likes activities involving strategy, rather than those involving physical force.

3 Letters on the Physical Plane: At times avoids facing reality, and instead creates an illusion. Can be careless and scattered about work and system; able to get a concept very quickly but does not want to be bothered by details. Likes variety in all things. Talented and artistic in whatever is undertaken. A strong sexual drive; freely discusses sexual matters. May have problems with reproductive organs; if so, it could be related to an emphasis on sexuality rather than creativity. Likes to dress "creatively" and be a little outrageous.

4 Letters on the Physical Plane: Not original or a true executive, however can easily carry out the ideas of others. Can be a workaholic; likes the order, system, and structure of the workplace. Takes work very seriously and can pay too much attention to details without getting the job completed smoothly. May be lazy and uncoordinated. Can be stubborn about alternative work procedures. May treat the sexual as work; therefore can be extremely conventional and have great difficulty dealing with a partner's demands.

5 *Letters on the Physical Plane:* Likes to travel. Will be successful if work involves contact with the public. Likes to regulate people and affairs. Restless when required to follow a routine. Good salesperson if convinced of product's worth. May seek escape in drugs, alcohol, gambling, or sex. Is sexually motivated (needs constant physical contact); may be promiscuous. Bad nerves may create sexual problem.

6 *Letters on the Physical Plane:* Likes to help others with things that require physical exertion. Can be very artistically inclined. A natural teacher or counselor, with the ability to make people feel that they are appreciated. Has good common sense. Gives comfort (has a strong maternal/paternal instinct). May exhibit poor taste in clothing and in home decoration. Physically somewhat frail because of worrying about things too much. Can be overly sentimental (could be perceived as moody). Sexually, will seem somewhat passive but can actually be very demanding and manipulative; not interested without feeling love is somehow involved.

7 *Letters on the Physical Plane:* Ill at ease in either public positions or positions of leadership; tends to avoid crowds, noise, and confusion. Can exhibit a great deal of self-control and dignity. Has some peculiar personality traits, such as being stingy, rude, demanding, and not very socially inclined or friendly. Selective in their choices of jobs and friends. Sometimes rigidity leads to missed opportunities. Very drawn to math and science. May be drawn toward a vocational field of interest. Sexually, needs love and understanding; may be more interested in receiving demonstrative affection

```
1 2 3 4 5 6 7 8 9
A B C D E F G H I
J K L M N O P Q R
S T U V W X Y Z
```

76   The Planes of Expression

(abandonment issues) than in reciprocating. May be interested in unusual or fantasy-related sexual activities.

8 Letters on the Physical Plane: Ambitious for power, position, and authority; is able to handle "big" things. Very competitive. Very good at using other people's money to make money, while holding on to own funds. Can be a good athlete. Wants recognition so badly is sometimes willing to be dishonest or greedy to achieve it. Very direct in sexual matters, thus might appear to others as ruthless or callous. Sexually, doesn't consider foreplay or romance; is either ready or unwilling to be bothered. May have serious sexual hang-ups (may role-play in an effort to figure out who is dominant in the relationship).

9 Letters on the Physical Plane: A dramatic flourish is always potentially present. Career choices may lean toward acting, poetry, music, and so on. May surround self with radical or unconventional friends or associates. Can often be impractical. Sexually, can be very warm and emotional. An appearance of emotional detachment may be a result of emotional scars from a previous relationship or a sexual problem from the past. Inclined to try to manipulate others through sex.

0 Letters on the Physical Plane: Prefers dreaming about accomplishments rather than physically accomplishing them. Works extremely hard to avoid work because of a dislike of getting hands dirty. Sexually, can become quickly disillusioned, bored, and disinterested.

Emotional Plane Interpretations
The total number of letters on this plane reveals how a person behaves in intimate relationships. Four or more letters on the emotional plane indicates a fiery temper.

1 Letter on the Emotional Plane: Very original. Capable of meeting all kinds of people. Can be nervous, very high-strung, sometimes fickle, or unreliable. Can be counted on to act "macho" (put on a rough exterior.) Demands much attention but is not very giving in return because of distrusting own feelings. A real game player. Can be selfish or full of self-pity.

2 Letters on the Emotional Plane: Can be codependent, needs to be loved. Needs to pay attention to the physical environment because of tendency to physically tune in to the energy or people around. Moods can change based on the atmosphere of the group. Has a good musical sense; attuned to rhythm and timing. Most likely to be a musician or make a living in music if this number is paired with either 3 or 9 on the physical plane. Always likes to share with others; needs companionship. May worry excessively. Can be difficult to help because of withholding expressions of disagreement or discomfort until the timing feels right. Easily hurt by criticism, so comments or assessments of others are often withheld. May become impulsively angry and "lash out" critically at others, with surprising intensity.

3 Letters on the Emotional Plane: Can be very talkative, sometimes too much so. Covets popularity and admiration. Emotionally, needs an artistic outlet, such as listening to music while working. Usually untidy and at the same time vain about personal dress and belongings (for example, may parade down the street all dressed up, having left behind a room that looks like a battle zone).

4 Letters on the Emotional Plane: Likes to have work properly appreciated. Has a natural sense of form, function, and fit. Likes routine, structure, and practicality. May resent or be confrontational with authority. Temper can be an issue. Will cling like a bulldog to an emotional relationship (friends or lovers) as well as other possessions;

78 The Planes of Expression

```
1 2 3 4 5 6 7 8 9
A B C D E F G H I
J K L M N O P Q R
S T U V W X Y Z
```

finds it hard to "give things up." Very poor at remembering birthdays and anniversaries and in keeping appointments. Emotional hang-ups and inhibitions cause great discomfort in relationships unless there is a feeling of being in charge.

5 *Letters on the Emotional Plane:* Always wants to know what/how others are feeling, but does not necessarily like to get emotionally close because doesn't like to reveal own feelings. Can be overly frank and brusque and oftentimes misleads others concerning personal feelings. Can be very chameleon-like and look okay but not feel okay. May have unpredictable emotional outbursts. May like to take risks based on emotional drives such as sex, pleasure, and so on.

6 *Letters on the Emotional Plane:* Feelings revolve around family, home, security. Honest and true. Can be irritable and cranky when ideals are not met. High expectations of/for others or self can make both parties unhappy and frustrated. Can be a bit of a hypochondriac because of emotional makeup. Gets "touchy" over certain personal issues. Has a great memory for embarrassing experiences (remembers incidents far too long). Can be manipulated through flattery, especially if this is the highest number on the planes of expression.

7 *Letters on the Emotional Plane:* Can be very thoughtful, selective, reserved, and secretive. Somewhat repressed emotionally (apprehension about opening up and either being abandoned, betrayed, or misunderstood). May appear aloof as has difficulty establishing new friendships. Will talk when certain of the subject matter and sure those listening are interested. Has a tendency to stay in the background at social functions and to limit time at functions unless something is of particular interest. Needs to learn to express inner feelings.

8 Letters on the Emotional Plane: Wants to dominate relationships. Can be very stubborn. Tries very hard to never have to admit to mistakes. Doesn't like having to learn things. May try very hard to avoid any spiritual growth and take a very pragmatic approach to life. Wants everything to conform to personal wishes. Fights usually occur over the other person's mistakes. Can have a bad temper that is extremely unpredictable. Potentially abusive in relationships, especially if 8 on the emotional plane is combined with 4 on the physical plane. Tends not to be romantic. May want to role-play the part of a prostitute, madam, or pimp. Very competitive in all areas of life, including love life and relationships. Love affairs are quite often associated with career advancement in some way. While having financial difficulties, sex is out of the question. Always sees good appearance as essential; would spend last dime on a shoeshine or new clothes just to appear successful.

9 Letters on the Emotional Plane: Overly dramatic. A bleeding heart, will stop people on the street and tell them a sad story. Emotions can swing from high to low with no apparent provocation. Very easily hurt and can be teary-eyed much of the time. Capable of success in any career as long as emotions can be controlled. Likes the admiration of crowds and groups; good on stage. Often blames others for own problems; overly complaining. Has difficulty expressing personal feelings. Cries even when angry, thereby making it hard for others to know true feelings.

0 Letters on the Emotional Plane: Lacks sympathy, patience, or tolerance. Being overly sentimental, can appear to be moody. Sexually, will appear passive but is actually very demanding and resourceful. Will engage in sexual activity when in love.

80   The Planes of Expression

1	2	3	4	5	6	7	8	9
A	B	C	D	E	F	G	H	I
J	K	L	M	N	O	P	Q	R
S	T	U	V	W	X	Y	Z	

Intuitive Plane Interpretations

1 Letter on the Intuitive Plane: Intuition hits like a bolt of lightning. Original ideas need to be made a reality. This number is a sign that this individual will not always listen to the inner self and thereby experiences growth via pain and sorrow that was avoidable.

2 Letters on the Intuitive Plane: Needs to learn to trust gut-level (intuitive) feelings, which may help solve personal conflicts and give clues as to how cooperation with others can be improved. Psychic; has many inner revelations. Often very in tune with surroundings; finds it difficult to understand why others do not feel or see the same.

3 Letters on the Intuitive Plane: Operates naturally with illusion (doesn't always accept the reality of a situation). An optimistic, wistful approach fosters the ability to inspire others to higher levels. Not very interested in accumulating wealth; doesn't care about the real value of money; sees money as being like a ticket to an amusement park. Can inspire others to be less rigid in their approach to life. Can talk a good game, but doesn't always follow through. Artistically inclined and may have good voice quality as either a speaker or singer. Biggest single hang-up and block to fully developing talent is a sexual hang-up. Underlying feelings of inadequacy may lead to taking personally something verbally directed at someone else. Can be concerned about "performance" in physical relationships.

4 Letters on the Intuitive Plane: Very pragmatic concerning intuition or mystical experiences. Not just hesitant about discussing or getting involved in these subjects, has a strong bias against anything that is not provable. More inventive than artistic. Likes solving problems. Due to a high degree of intuition, often unused, able to figure a way out of a predicament with what are believed to be logical and practical solutions. May wonder at times where the information came from. Prefers conventional religions, those steeped in tradition and ceremony. Able to be a good orthodox anything.

5 *Letters on the Intuitive Plane:* Is very attuned and could get most any kind of insight wished, but can be skeptical about intuition. Can be somewhat pragmatic; sometimes wonders about knowledge coming without proper training or education, but does accept insights. May seem to be reading others' minds. Can know the motives of new acquaintances and friends after just a few seconds of conversation. "Knows" what people are up to; can read people at their soul level. May have difficulty with formal learning because of boredom. Learns best by using the powers of observation, through hands-on experience or through life experiences. Could easily become a jack-of-all-trades and master of none.

6 *Letters on the Intuitive Plane:* Apt to experience a psychic, intuitive, spiritual breakthrough sometime in life regarding the best way to serve humankind. Tendency to see self as doing big things, but seldom makes plans a reality because of unrealistic expectations and perfectionist tendencies. May have visions of grandeur. Doesn't want to be an important, leader type. More comfortable in the role of mother or father to the world. Sensitive to injustice; wants fairness and equality for everyone. Will likely experience a great many disappointments in life because of putting people on pedestals. Can become easily discouraged and disappointed. If a mother/father role is adopted in a relationship, the relationship will not be fulfilling because its basis is codependency. Feels others aren't dependable; tries to assume responsibility and may become a caretaker. The drive to take care of or assist others can generate a "martyr" role. Can bond quickly and may have brief but intense relationships.

7 Letters on the Intuitive Plane: Automatically *knows.* Is naturally psychic. Can become an occultist or study metaphysics. Has a very analytical mind and likes to probe the abstract. Knows there is an answer for everything, but just hasn't found it yet. (Would make a good numerologist.) Combines artistic talent (3) with inventive talent (4), therefore can be either or both. Can become a crusader, inventor, artist, spiritual leader, or a hermit.

8 Letters on the Intuitive Plane: Uses intuition and insight to further personal aims. Has a need/drive to be in charge at church, lodge, or metaphysical organization.

9 Letters on the Intuitive Plane: Can inspire others to do great things. Extremely idealistic and impressionable but not always practical. May have a tendency to go off in a daze or daydream. From time to time opportunities will arise, making the influence of a great many people possible.

0 Letters on the Intuitive Plane: Distrusts own intuition. When seeking answers to bigger problems, may resort to prayer, meditation, or consciousness-expanding techniques . . . especially after the mid-life crisis.

A Very Quick Snapshot

The first letter of a name can provide you with an instant insight into a person's approach, based on the planes of expression. The first letter of the first or middle name can reveal a primary approach to dealing with the world at large. The first name relates to work and the physical world, and the middle name reflects the emotional self as well as how it approaches relationships. The first letter of a last name can reveal either a positive or negative approach to family decision making.

1. Circle the first letter of the first name:
    Mental approach to decision making: A, G, H, J, L, N, P

Physical approach to decision making: E, D, M, W

Emotional approach to decision making: B, I, O, R, S, T, X, Z

Intuitive approach to decision making: C, F, K, Q, U, V, Y

2. Circle the first letter of the middle name:

   Mental approach to decision making: A, G, H, J, L, N, P

   Physical approach to decision making: E, D, M, W

   Emotional approach to decision making: B, I, O, R, S, T, X, Z

   Intuitive approach to decision making: C, F, K, Q, U, V, Y

3. Circle the first letter of the last name:

   Mental approach to decision making: A, G, H, J, L, N, P

   Physical approach to decision making: E, D, M, W

   Emotional approach to decision making: B, I, O, R, S, T, X, Z

   Intuitive approach to decision making: C, F, K, Q, U, V, Y

6

Bringing It All Together

Applying Cosmic Numerology at
Work and at Home

Now you are fully equipped to use numerology in whatever situation you find yourself. A few settings are presented here, with several examples that demonstrate how the methods presented in the earlier chapters can be applied to foster effective business transactions and management, enhance instructive and therapeutic relationships, and improve family dynamics.

USING NUMEROLOGY TO SUCCESSFULLY COMPETE IN BUSINESS

Gaining an advantage over your competition is one of the most important aspects of success in business. Whether a client or potential client is an individual or a business, you can gain an advantage through your knowledge of the client's behavior patterns, preferences, and modes of communication. Successful business managers do not wait for knowledge to come to them; they pursue it. Numerology provides a very convenient way to do this.

```
1 2 3 4 5 6 7 8 9
A B C D E F G H I
J K L M N O P Q R
S T U V W X Y Z
```
Bringing It All Together   **85**

For example: Microsoft is soliciting bids for a project they are about to initiate. Many of your competitors are bidding on the same project. How do you propose something unique? Using the knowledge gained from this book and your own research, your presentation could be developed with your knowledge of Microsoft's emotional and psychological approach to business and to life. By combining the insights derived from the V/CC of the company name (detailed in chapter 4) and the achievement number (detailed in chapter 2), you will be well guided.

First Name V/CC: Microsoft
- Find the numeric equivalent of the first consonant, *M,* which is 4.
- Next, find the numeric equivalent of the first vowel, *I,* which is 9.
- Add the consonant total of 4 to the vowel total of 9 for a sum of 13. Reduce the 13 by adding 1 + 3 = 4. Write the answer as 4/.
- Next, subtract the consonant total of 4 from the vowel total of 9 for a result of 5.
- Write the final equation as 4/5.

With a 13 under the surface, this company may be skeptical about outsiders, and the 4/5 says it does not like change (5) unless it is doing the changing (4). The *M* as the first letter indicates it knows how to manipulate (a statement, not a judgment).

Achievement Number
(Achievement number based on the date of reincorporation in Delaware, September 22, 1993.)
- 9 + 22 = 31; 31 reduced is 3 + 1 = 4; resulting in an AN of 31/4
- Positive: Innovative (1), visionary (3), making visions into reality (4)
- Negative: Arrogant (1), unforgiving (3), stubborn (4)

Control is a major issue for achievement number 4, as is procrastination. This business likes order, system, and structure. It feels it should be "the boss" and that its way is the best way. Its main issue is to build a solid foundation and not to take short cuts, procrastinate, be judgmental, be stubborn, be prejudicial, or get lost in minutiae. It is a business that is well organized and gets things done, with a natural affinity for form, fit, and function.

Interpretations for the 31 of the 31/4 (based on the basic number concepts and positive and negative attributes of numbers detailed in chapter 1):

1 • Issues of the Ego Self
   Positive: Self-directed, leader, paradigm buster, innovator, assertive, energetic, balanced, follows internal guidance, an initiator, comfortable with self
   Negative: Passive, aggressive, egocentric, low self-esteem, fearful, timid, arrogant, a zealot, a bully, no sense of self

3 • Issues Involving Communication, Social Interactions,
   Feelings of Inadequacy
   Positive: Joyful, witty, artistic, charismatic, charming, creative, intelligent, optimistic, a communicator, extrovert, visionary, musician, good sense of humor—likes to laugh
   Negative: Moody/emotional, unforgiving, scattered, an introvert, exaggerates, vain, feelings of inferiority or inadequacy, leaves things unfinished, sarcastic, grandiose plans, jealousy, concerned about being judged, temperamental, ill-tempered, a bit of a gossip

Combining AN and V/CC = 31/4 and 4/5

The AN indicates ego issues (1) with own creations (3) and control of their use (4). Unless this company can determine which changes will occur and when (5), it becomes overly cautious and a little stubborn (4) when it comes to making changes.

Analysis Based on First Name Total = 46/1 (see chapter 4)

1 • Likes to be the initiator, the leader. May like to work alone. Emphatic.

6 • Likes to serve, counsel, and advise in any capacity. Can be perfectionist. May take on too much responsibility or want to advise but not assume responsibility. Confidant for others.

4 • Wants order, system, and structure. May "go by the book." May get lost in minutiae. Is logical and may want to be the "boss." Can be somewhat stubborn and a tad confrontational.

Synopsis of Microsoft Data

The underlying 13 of the V/CC creates a mirror pattern with the foundation number of the AN, 31. This company has the opportunity to become either an innovative visionary that can change reality, a positive 31, or a second-rate negative 13 with a culture that may be unforgiving, scattered, skeptical, arrogant, grandiose, or fixated on its own solutions (4).

This company will be interested in submissions that use an inside-out approach. Start with their data and turn it inside out by offering an innovative (not creative) solution that melds with their love of innovation.

HUMAN RESOURCE APPLICATIONS

Human resource departments can use these formulas to:
- Build stronger and more compatible teams: teams combined of individuals with complementary talents instead of conflicting behaviors increase loyalty, job satisfaction, and productivity, and minimize bickering, dissention, and malingering.
- Resolve/neutralize conflicts more quickly.
- Better understand group dynamics: whether the group is composed

```
1 2 3 4 5 6 7 8 9
A B C D E F G H I
J K L M N O P Q R
S T U V W X Y Z
```

88   Bringing It All Together

of senior management or a work team of four part-time employees, it is vital to the group's success that tasks are assigned according to individuals' strengths. Familiarity with the material in this book can facilitate teaming decisions.

- Enable participants in employee assistance programs to identify and begin changing reactive behavior patterns: whatever problem(s) the employee is experiencing (relationships, stress, alcohol or drug use, or mental health issues), his or her ability to gain knowledge of basic emotional and psychological behavior patterns can facilitate a quicker transformation to new and more positive behavior patterns.

- Facilitate better employee communication and interaction by "hearing" what employees have to say and understanding their emotional components.

- Assist employees to find their "happy spot" within the organization. Is there anyone more productive and satisfied than someone who is doing what he or she loves?

FOR SALESPERSONS

Cosmic Numerology can easily be used to identify a client's behavior patterns and tailor a presentation to increase the probability of a sale. Suppose you sell big-ticket items like manufacturing or construction equipment, automobiles, homes, or home appliances. If you know the person's first name, you can correctly tailor your presentation in less than sixty seconds, based on insights into thought and behavior patterns.

Analysis Based on First Letter of First Name

Use the first letter of the first name to uncover his or her primary approach to dealing with the world at large, then correlate it with the planes of expression:

Mental approach to decision making: A, G, H, J, L, N, P

Physical approach to decision making (a tire kicker): E, D, M, W

Emotional approach to decision making: B, I, O, R, S, T, X, Z

Intuitive approach to decision making: C, F, K, Q, U, V, Y

Analysis Based on First Name V/CC and First Name Total

Aaron   *V/CC 2/9*   *First name total = 22/4*

Takes a mental approach. Can either bend over backward to be accommodating (2/9) if he needs preapproval for his actions (22/4), or wants to control the situation (2/9) because he knows the way it ought to be (22/4). The double *A* can make him mentally stubborn.

Abigail   *V/CC 3/1*   *First name total = 32/5*

Takes a mental approach. May start as a "window shopper" (3/1), but to please others (2) and liking the finer things in life (3), may make an impulsive decision (5). As much as she wants the freedom to do what she wants, when she wants, with whomever she wants (5), she may "check in" with someone else prior to making a decision (2) because of feelings of inadequacy (3).

Barbara   *V/CC 3/1*   *First name total = 25/7*

Takes an emotional approach. May start as a "window shopper" (3/1) wishing for or desiring something, but low self-esteem (1) and feelings of inadequacy (3) combined with not wanting to make a mistake or be embarrassed (7) may cause her either to be unable to make a decision or to walk away.

Benjamin   *V/CC 7/3*   *First name total = 32/5*

Takes an emotional approach. Can be impatient or sarcastic if he feels the salesperson is not sufficiently knowledgeable about the product (7/3). May be overconfident and get agitated or sarcastic with those who do not appreciate his knowledge (7/3). May not trust his intuition (2)

and thus be attracted to something that "glitters" (3), which he "has" to have, resulting in an impulse purchase (5).

Carlos   *V/CC 4/2*   *First name total = 23/5*

Takes an intuitive approach. Likes to see himself as independent and seldom relies on others (4/2). However, with feelings of inadequacy under the surface (3), he can be influenced by others or ignore all advice (2) and act impulsively (5).

Elizabeth   *V/CC 8/2*   *First name total = 43/7*

Takes a physical approach. May appear to be "imperial" (8) at times because she expects others to know or anticipate what she wants (2) without having to tell them. Likes to be complimented on her physical appearance or her intelligence (the 8 and 7 combined with the insecurity of the 3).

FOR MENTAL HEALTH PROFESSIONALS AND SOCIAL WORKERS

Mental health professionals and social workers can use the achievement number and V/CC to rapidly establish a connection by verbally identifying the client's behavior patterns, underlying motivations, and core issues. I work with adolescents; this technique gets their attention very quickly.

Mental health issues can have their seeds in our middle names as well as in our achievement numbers. Our middle name represents our emotional approach to life, how we interact with others, the kinds of people we are attracted to, and how we behave in relationships.

- Middle name single-digit totals of 1, 2, 6, 7, or 9 may indicate co-dependency issues.
- Middle name single-digit totals of 1, 4, 5, 7, 8, and 9 may indicate control issues.

```
1 2 3 4 5 6 7 8 9
A B C D E F G H I
J K L M N O P Q R
S T U V W X Y Z
```

Bringing It All Together **91**

- Someone without a middle name has chosen to learn to balance his or her emotions, which can have sharp peaks and deep valleys.
- There are clues in a full numerology chart where an analysis of the relationships between the complete name; the month, day, and year of birth; and specific challenges and *soulutions* reveals how the person can best balance his or her emotions.

Analysis Based on Middle Name V/CC and Middle Name Total

Ann   *V/CC 2/9*   *Middle name total = 11/2*

The V/CC of 2/9 shows a pattern of being overly accommodating, and the 11/2 indicates a need to "make things right"; relationships may involve trying to fix "broken wings." Ultimately, the relationship will end by her either being abandoned or by her learning to let go of emotional and sentimental attachments (that is, staying long after she should have left).

Edward   *V/CC 9/1*   *Middle name total = 28/1*

This combination indicates a person who will do for others, if he chooses (9/1), and who could be somewhat passive-aggressive emotionally (28). The first letter, *E,* combined with the name total of 1 can indicate a need for physical contact (hugging, touching, kissing, holding hands). If he is a strong 28/1, he will push to have things his way, while if he is weak, he will acquiesce to the demands of others.

Jessica   *V/CC 6/4*   *Middle name total = 21/3*

The *E* as the first vowel but not the first letter indicates that before allowing physical intimacy she will make her partner perform the "twelve feats of Hercules," twelve impossible tasks to prove himself worthy of being with her. She is also susceptible to being seduced by flattery. The 6/4 V/CC indicates she will take on a partner's responsibilities (6) in addition to her own because of a tendency to be a mother figure in a relationship. The 21/3 shows she is a romantic (3) but does not speak

1	2	3	4	5	6	7	8	9
A	B	C	D	E	F	G	H	I
J	K	L	M	N	O	P	Q	R
S	T	U	V	W	X	Y	Z	

92   Bringing It All Together

her emotional truths (3) because of a lack of confidence (1) and over-sensitivity to the input of others (2). She fails to consistently speak her feelings (3), so something inconsequential can set her off like a small thermonuclear bomb. The *A* as the last letter can indicate regrets caused by not listening to her intuition.

Linda   *V/CC 3/6*   *Middle name total = 22/4*

Has a tendency to take on too much responsibility (6) and scatter her energies (3). With *A* as the last letter, there can be regrets caused by not listening to her intuition. The 22/4 brings the dual energy of a need for preapproval by others (2) and defiance of authority if she thinks she is right (4.)

Richard   *V/CC 9/9*   *Middle name total = 43/7*

The 9/9 indicates intensity, and the 43/7 reveals feelings of inade-quacy (3) and a need to be in control (4) because of abandonment issues (7). He can be on everyone's short list as a lover due to being a great giver; however, he may be afraid to receive, fearing what is given may be withdrawn, or he may be cold and distant—self-contained.

Rodriguez   *V/CC 6/3*   *Middle name total = 60/6*

The V/CC of 6/3 indicates he can be unforgiving toward those he feels do not appreciate his sacrifices. He can also be sarcastic (3) when trying to get others to be personally responsible (6). The 60/6 can be reflected in behavior that is controlling because *he* knows best. *R* as the first letter brings intensity, and the second letter, *O,* brings perfection-ist tendencies and unrealistic expectations of self and others. This can manifest as health issues in the digestive system.

Stephen   *V/CC 8/2*   *Middle name total = 33/6*

The *S* indicates he is seldom satisfied emotionally and constantly strives to make things better. He may avoid stepping into his power (8) because of the influence of others, or he will do for others (2) because of feelings of inadequacy (33) and a sense of responsibility that can lead to martyrdom (33/6.) *E* as the first vowel indicates his emotions can impact his nervous system leading to health issues.

Susan   *V/CC 4/2*   *Middle name total = 11/2*

The *S* indicates she is seldom satisfied emotionally, and the *U* can lead to unexpressed frustration, which leads to the second *S* and further dissatisfaction that can manifest itself as health issues involving the head and neck or upper back as well as eyes, ears, nose, throat, teeth, sinuses, or headaches (*A*). The V/CC of 4/2 indicates she finds others to be unreliable and feels she has to do everything herself. With a first name total of 11/2, she may be attracted to people she feels need her help and then find the relationships unsatisfying.

FOR HEALTH PRACTITIONERS

Health practitioners can get a thumbnail sketch of a patient's emotional and psychological behavior patterns in less than a minute. These behaviors are also part of an overall pattern that is the catalyst for specific health issues (e.g., illnesses, diseases, and injuries). It is my belief that the proportion of negative to positive energy in our bodies increases in direct proportion to the intensity of our abandonment/separation issues. Every time we do something to be loved or to maintain control, we pump one additional particle of negative energy into our bodies. As the proportion of negative particles increases, so does the probability of developing health issues. The illnesses, diseases, and injuries we are most prone to manifest match the numbers of our various challenges. Using the *Table of Challenges and Soulutions* (on page 38) and the positive and negative interpretations of the numbers 1 through 9 as represented by the achievement numbers, V/CC challenges, and the planes of expression, practitioners can quickly identify some of the catalysts for a health issue.

In my book *Numerology for Healing* (Destiny Books, 2009), I

```
1 2 3 4 5 6 7 8 9
A B C D E F G H I
J K L M N O P Q R
S T U V W X Y Z
```

94   Bringing It All Together

identify the relationships among more than two hundred illnesses and diseases and the reactive behavior patterns that were their catalysts. My work is currently being used by naturopathic physicians, homeopaths, physical therapists, chiropractors, acupuncturists, psychiatrists, and social workers to augment their expertise in their modality. In the following examples, excerpted from that book, the letters of the condition's name are transposed to a numeric sum, shown in parentheses.

Anxiety (35/8)

Fear of the physical world (5), feelings of inadequacy (3), and difficulty with personal empowerment can bring on mental, emotional, even physical paralysis. The individual doesn't want to risk making an incorrect decision, so he or she won't move (in any direction). Anxiety is also associated with abandonment issues.

The V/CC of *AN* is 6/4, which is associated with issues involving control and responsibility.

Drug Problems (60/6)

Those with drug problems face issues of personal responsibility and unrealistic expectations of self and others, which lead to disappointment and a desire to escape the current reality. There are issues of anxiety and difficulty involving "close" relationships with others (6). The abuse of a drug (23/5) is the result of poor communication skills (2), feelings of inadequacy (3), and an inability to function in the physical world (5) due to unrealistic expectations (6).

The V/CC of *DRU* results in 7/1, indicating issues of self-esteem and abandonment.

Frigidity (62/8)

Communication issues (2) combined with perfectionist tendencies (6) result in power issues (8): Who's in charge? Who has the power? The numbers 2 and 6 also deal with relationships and issues of vulnerability. Look at the negative characteristics of the achievement numbers:

1	2	3	4	5	6	7	8	9
A	B	C	D	E	F	G	H	I
J	K	L	M	N	O	P	Q	R
S	T	U	V	W	X	Y	Z	

Bringing It All Together **95**

2 (interactions with others), 6 (martyrdom and family issues), and 8 (issues dealing with personal power). Also look for insights in the planes of expression.

The V/CC of *FRI* is 6/3, indicating a lack of communication and feelings of inadequacy, combined with a possible unconscious lack of forgiveness toward a family member or person from a previous relationship.

Stiff (24/6) Neck (15/6) = (39/12/3)

Because both *stiff* and *neck* transpose to the number 6, the main issues involve maintaining unrealistic expectations of self (1) or others and a stubbornness (4) or rigidity (5) when it comes to interacting with others (2) or doing things differently. The 3s on either side of the 39/12/3 reveal that feelings of inadequacy are the catalyst for neck stiffness. The 2 indicates difficulty with cooperation or compromise. The 1 points to the self as the center of the equation, and the 9 reflects difficulty letting go or changing directions (because this may conflict with being loved or maintaining control of a situation).

The V/CC of *STI* is 3/6, indicating unrealistic expectations and lack of communication (i.e., emotional intimacy).

FOR EDUCATORS

I have an M.Ed. in special education and have been a special education teacher for over twenty-five years. I've also taught in colleges and private schools and have been a corporate trainer. I practice what I preach every day. We became educators because we wanted to make a difference in people's lives; what greater difference can we make than to give our students self-knowledge and encouragement to fulfill their potential?

As early as possible in the school year or as soon as I can after they enter my class, I will have a talk with my students after privately analyzing their numbers. I will show them how to maximize their strengths and recognize what pushes their buttons. For most of my students, this is the first time anyone has pointed out their strengths. My goal is to have them use this self-knowledge to invest in themselves and bring more abundance and happiness into their lives. With my principal's permission, I have started a numerology club at the high school where I teach.

Educators are expected to individualize their presentation of classroom materials. This can be very difficult if not impossible with twenty-five to thirty-five students in a class, taking attendance, stopping for PA announcements, classroom distractions, and unprepared students. The solution is to have a tool that allows you to cut to the quick of any behavioral or academic challenges. Once you become proficient using the formulas of this book, you should be able to identify basic behavior patterns and life approaches in less than sixty seconds. This can readily be done with the first and middle name analyses shown in the examples given in the sections on sales and for mental health professionals and social workers.

FOR FAMILIES

Parents and grandparents can help maximize a child's strengths by helping him or her make more proactive decisions and fewer reactive decisions. Working with a child to help him change his achievement number from being a core challenge to becoming a core strength is an investment that will pay him lifelong dividends.

It is the parent's responsibility to help shape the child as a human being: to teach her to communicate her feelings, to understand the consequences of her actions, to take personal responsibility, to laugh at herself, to ask questions, and above all, to develop the courage and persistence to pursue her dreams.

I believe our children consciously chose us to be their parents. It is our responsibility to teach them how to think and reason; make conscious choices; laugh and giggle; be curious about life, adventurous, compassionate, ethical, creative, sensitive to the needs of others; and yet to be assertive. If we teach our children from our heart, we can become children again.

Becoming familiar with your child's "numbers" will enable you to encourage and guide him toward maximizing his strengths and converting reactive behavior patterns into conscious, proactive choices. Remember, each of us has guaranteed ourselves success; we have provided a soulution for every challenge. Use the *Table of Challenges and Soulutions* presented in chapter 3 for yourself and your child; it is your roadmap to an abundant life.

Conclusion

In the introduction I wrote, "The purpose of this book is to assist you to better understand some of the underlying causes of reactive behavior patterns, whether in yourself or others." Has it helped you better understand these reactive behavior patterns? I hope so. Using just the interpretations for the achievement numbers and the V/CC challenges, the core issues and strengths of anyone or anything can be understood. Proficiency in using this knowledge enables businesses and individuals in their capacity as salespeople, human resource personnel, health practitioners, teachers, social workers, or parents and grandparents to better understand themselves and those whom they serve or with whom they relate. My intention in writing this book was to present a more concise way to understand why we do what we do at work, in relationships, and with family by combining the insights provided by the first, middle, and last names combined with the month and day of birth.

I have discovered that some V/CC combinations occur much more frequently than others. Those combinations are: 2/1, 3/1, 7/1, 9/1, 4/2, 8/2, 9/2, 5/3, 6/3, 7/3, 9/3, 5/4, 6/4, 4/5, 7/5, and 8/6. If you focus on familiarizing yourself with these combinations and become adept in applying the positive and negative concepts associated with the numbers 1 through 9, you will successfully identify anyone's V/CC and achievement number behavior patterns in less than sixty seconds. Here are a few examples:

- V/CC of 2/9: the negative 9 may result in the person doing to be loved or to maintain control. Someone with a negative 2 can be either insensitive or overly sensitive when interacting with others. What is the person's body language saying—codependent or controlling?

- V/CC of 5/8: the person could have issues involving power (8), influencing the 5 toward rigidity.

- V/CC of 5/6: the person could be overly involved in the issues of others (6), leading to difficulty with change or movement (5).

The defining factor in determining how to interpret a V/CC is the use of the achievement number(s). The achievement number (AN) identifies a person's reactive core issue(s). People with an AN of 25/7 may be apprehensive about change (5) and may have difficulty interacting with others (2), coupled with a need to be validated for their usefulness (7).

As you ponder your reactive behavior patterns or those of others, try to keep in mind that we are all going through various phases of personal growth. I visualize human beings moving through four growth phases. We may move through all four phases in a single lifetime or multiple lifetimes; it depends on how quickly personal consciousness is attained and practiced. The four phases are:

- *Phase 1—We Do Unto Others (Ego).* We live a life with no consequences for our actions. We murder, lie, cheat, steal, plunder, pillage, rape, burn, torture, and indulge our wildest fantasies.

- *Phase 2—Others Do Unto Us (Ego).* Whether we were aware of it or not, we had reciprocal agreements with those we victimized in Phase 1. In Phase 2, those IOUs are paid back. We are murdered, lied to, cheated on, stolen from, plundered, pillaged, raped, burned, tortured, or are the recipient of indulged fantasies. At this point we can become angry, indignant, and seek revenge. We have three options: return to

Phase 1, remain in Phase 2 as a "victim," or go to Phase 3. If we want to pay back what was done to us, we will return to Phase 1, to again become trapped in a karmic cycle of "doing to and being done to."

- *Phase 3—Acceptance of What Is/Was/Will Be.* Phase 3 is about potential: a potential for reunification of the ego and the soul and evolving to Phase 4, or the potential to revert to Phase 1 and to "do unto others." If we accept that we chose the role of victim in Phase 2 to balance out our role as perpetrator in Phase 1, we can break out of the karmic cycle of reactive behaviors and shatter the illusion of cosmic abandonment. We begin to have a sense that there is more to existence than what we are able to perceive with our physical senses. We begin an inner journey of self-discovery, leading us to examine our lives, our decisions, and the consequences of those decisions. We want to know who we are and why are we here. We are ready to go to Phase 4.

- *Phase 4—Integrating Our Ego and Our Soul.* In this phase we reintegrate our ego and soul.

Until we reach Phase 4, the ego can sabotage the soul's attempts to remember it chose to be here, rather than being sent here. The ego's abandonment issues are evident every time we do something out of fear, whether it's due to codependent actions or actions that give the illusion of being in control. More often than not, the soul tries to ignore the ego and its fear-based decisions. It feels its divineness and wants to reconnect with Source. It believes that the ego holds it back and therefore tries to ignore ego-based feelings and emotions. This attitude drives a wedge between the ego and the soul. The ego, feeling abandoned and ignored by the soul, sabotages the soul's desire for reconnection with creation.

I can best explain this with a picture. We've all seen the cartoon where a dog is enticed to chase another animal and just as it is about to catch it, he reaches the end of his leash and is suddenly jerked backward. The same situation applies to us. We may commit ourselves to the spiritual path and pursue it with determination and single-minded focus. Everything seems to fall into place when, all of a sudden, we are jerked backward. Stunned at the sudden change, we question Spirit. We are confused, even angry; haven't we been doing everything required of us? Yes, we have. But, in the process, we have neglected an important aspect of our self—the ego. It was the ego that jerked on the chain to remind the soul that this is a partnership and that the ego will no longer be ignored.

How do we get the soul and ego to work together? Try this exercise:

1. Find a quiet place where you will not be disturbed by others or by the sounds of electrical devices. Sit down and close your eyes.

2. Slowly inhale through your nose for a count of five. Hold this breath for a count of five and then slowly exhale through your lips for a count of five. Repeat this three times.

3. When you feel relaxed, visualize being inside your body.

4. As a third party (your essence), acknowledge the presence of the ego and then recognize the presence of the soul. Mentally project them out of your head into a space where they can sit across from each other. Speaking to both at the same time, invite them to join you in a dialog about their relationship. Ask the ego to explain its reasons for sabotaging the soul whenever it tries to soar or ask if it feels the soul gives it enough respect. Ask the ego about its abandonment issues and if there is anything else it wants to discuss. Thank the ego for expressing its feelings.

5. Then ask the soul why it doesn't give the ego more respect. Ask the soul what could be more important than working in partnership with its physical aspect that helps ground it to the planet. Thank the soul. Thank them both for agreeing to form a conscious partnership.

6. Now direct them to speak with each other and reach a solution that will allow them to work as a team. While they are doing this, continue to observe as a third party. Once they reach a solution, thank them for their hard work and ask them to state what they have agreed on. Thank them again and then invite both back into your mental space, where the three of you meld into a single entity. This new self will have the courage to make decisions that will enable it to evolve to its highest potential.

Being aware of the four developmental phases and using the above exercise can enable us to make fewer reactive life choices and more conscious choices.

One final thought:

> *This above all: to thine own self be true,*
> *And it must follow, as the night the day,*
> *Thou canst not then be false to any man.*
>
> WILLIAM SHAKESPEARE,
> *HAMLET,* ACT I, SCENE 3

Table of Predefined 1st Vowel/1st Consonant Challenges (V/CC)

The following paragraphs describe the number combinations as they relate to the V/CC formulas. I have especially kept the definitions of the 1st vowel/1st consonant combinations brief. You will want to use your knowledge of the negative characteristics of the numbers 1 through 9 (see chapter 1) to expand on these interpretations. Being familiar with the meaning of the numbers will enhance your ability to determine whether or not someone has resolved his or her challenge issues.

COMBINATIONS WITH NUMBER 1
Issues of the Ego Self

Combinations with the number 1 involve issues of self-esteem. Interactions with others can be reflected through a lens smeared with a lack of confidence. This lack of confidence may be displayed as either arrogance or timidity.

2/1 Codependent on others for self-esteem; doesn't always speak up in a timely fashion due to oversensitivity; may display timidity or fear.

104   Appendix I

1	2	3	4	5	6	7	8	9
A	B	C	D	E	F	G	H	I
J	K	L	M	N	O	P	Q	R
S	T	U	V	W	X	Y	Z	

Notes on Using This Table

- Interpret these combinations from right to left.
- The key to using these definitions is to always keep in mind that the basic issues involved (indicated by the number to the right)—such as self-esteem (/1), cooperation and sensitivity (/2), self-confidence and communication (/3), and so on—overlay the negative characteristics of the vowel/consonant combination.
- Other than the combination of 9/9, there are no other combinations composed of the same number (e.g., 1/1, 2/2, 3/3). It is mathematically impossible.
- These combinations represent the blueprint an individual used to begin life. As he or she resolves challenges, they can be transmuted into strengths.

In combination with an achievement number of 1, 4, 5, or 8, this V/CC may indicate a person who places own interests above those of others.

3/1 Can be unforgiving of others when expectations are not met; may not always finish what is started (doesn't want to be judged); can be sarcastic. Feelings of insecurity can affect self-esteem. Can be a "window shopper" who enjoys looking at pretty things, human or merchandise, but seldom buys.

May suffer from a lack of confidence and tend to withdraw from the world, even become a recluse. A vivid imagination full of self-aggrandizing ideas, combined with false confidence or egocentrism, makes them more of a sideshow barker than someone grounded in reality.

4/1 Needs to be in control; can procrastinate; can be overly logical, getting lost in the minutiae; can bury self in work. Identity can be linked

```
1 2 3 4 5 6 7 8 9
A B C D E F G H I
J K L M N O P Q R
S T U V W X Y Z
```
Table of Predefined 1st Vowel/1st Consonant Challenges   105

to what he or she does, not who he or she is. May be stubborn due to a lack of confidence.

5/1 Can be inflexible and resistant to change or overly amenable with no sense of self. Change is "good" if under own control, "bad" if not. May be demanding and impulsive, propelled by own wishes.

6/1 Takes on responsibility to the point of martyrdom or may totally avoid responsibility; needs to give advice and counsel to others.

7/1 Finds it much easier to give than receive due to vulnerability issues; may appear aloof; may poke nose into the affairs of others to offer unsolicited advice. May be apprehensive about being in charge (doesn't want to make mistakes or be embarrassed) or may assume his or her way is the only way. Needs validation of usefulness, intelligence, compassion, and dedication (related to abandonment issues).

8/1 Money, status, power, and delegating to others are very important. Can become angry, frustrated, or disloyal if there is a perceived lack of recognition. May appear arrogant to cover feelings of inadequacy or low self-esteem.

9/1 Needs to be thanked, recognized, or appreciated for contributions or may ignore the needs of others and only do for self. May go through pain and suffering to open her heart. May consistently put others ahead of himself.

COMBINATIONS WITH NUMBER 2
Issues Involving Others

Combinations with the number 2 involve issues of cooperation, sensitivity, and timely communication. The catalyst for this pattern is the level of sensitivity displayed toward others. If there is too much sensitivity, these individuals will have difficulty with codependency issues. If there

106 Appendix I

```
1 2 3 4 5 6 7 8 9
A B C D E F G H I
J K L M N O P Q R
S T U V W X Y Z
```

is too little sensitivity, these individuals have a tendency to beat people between the eyes with the hammer of truth. (They need to put a little padding on that hammer.)

1/2 May be overly dependent on others for support and a sense of identity. May be egocentric as a defense against dependency on others. May have difficulty letting go of emotional and sentimental attachments due to a lack of confidence.

3/2 Relationships can be difficult due to feelings of insecurity, poor communication skills, or excessive optimism. May become sarcastic or unforgiving toward those perceived as unappreciative or not living up to expectations.

4/2 Probably has cold fingers and toes. Finds people to be inconsistent and unreliable, resulting in a tendency to put energy into work (likes the order, system, structure, and schedules of the workplace and could become/be a workaholic). Likes to maintain order, system, structure, and a schedule in personal life. Either loves to clean or hates it; when cleaning, needs to see concrete results (e.g., vacuuming up "dust bunnies" or scrubbing very dirty dishes or windows). Parents probably had a strict belief system. Whether parents were hippies or religious fundamentalists, they felt their way was the only way. Those with this combination may find it easier to give than receive.

May try to dominate others—mentally, emotionally, or physically.

5/2 Can be inflexible and refuse to cooperate with others. Timidity and difficulty dealing with change may make it difficult to interact with others. Timidity could be displayed by trying to accommodate everyone. A rigid or stubborn attitude can be a reflection of difficulty dealing with change.

6/2 Needs to give advice to others, whether it is wanted or not. There is a tendency toward a codependency, of needing to be needed, pos-

```
1 2 3 4 5 6 7 8 9
A B C D E F G H I
J K L M N O P Q R
S T U V W X Y Z
```
Table of Predefined 1st Vowel/1st Consonant Challenges   **107**

sibly more than those around her would need her . . . a potential martyr.

Another negative pattern could involve unrealistic expectations of self and others, making cooperation difficult.

A third pattern may be insensitivity to others and avoidance of personal responsibility.

7/2 Needs to be the "savior" and is hurt when others are not sufficiently appreciative. Has a need to be validated for insights, compassion, and usefulness to the group. Abandonment issues play a large part in decision making.

8/2 When this type of person walks into a room, he expects everyone else to know what he wants merely by inhaling the molecules he exhales. Definitely needs to work on communication skills and being less pompous.

9/2 Overly sensitive and emotional and finds it hard to let go (may have lower back pain or soreness/stiffness in neck area or joints). Dependent on receiving recognition, appreciation, and thanks for "good" deeds. Can be codependent. Will bend over backward to do for others until saturation point is reached; then just wants to be left alone and not disturbed.

COMBINATIONS WITH NUMBER 3
Issues Involving Communication, Social Interactions, Feelings of Inadequacy

Combinations with the number 3 involve issues of communication, social interactions, and feelings of adequacy. If the negative aspects of 3 are emphasized, can be flashy or withdrawn, sarcastic or noncommunicative, the life of the party or a wallflower, as well as being unforgiving, glib, scattered, moody, and indecisive, with a tendency to exaggerate, difficulty in finishing what is started, and a tendency to lean toward grandiosity.

1/3 Lack of self-confidence or moodiness can lead to low self-esteem. Can be unforgiving toward those perceived as nonsupportive. May exaggerate, be a gossip, or make grandiose plans.

2/3 Difficulty in relationships or social interactions due to a combination of oversensitivity, poor communication skills, and feelings of inadequacy. Because of a need for validation, may overcommit when offering to do for others.

4/3 Can be stubborn, procrastinate, or get lost in minutiae due to feelings of insecurity or inadequacy. May like to be in control of social interactions. Other potential negative patterns involve the use of sarcasm as a means to control.

5/3 Doesn't like change and can make things unpleasant for those trying to implement the change. Feelings of inadequacy concerning a new situation can be reflected in rigid behavior patterns. Often resists being forced into unfamiliar situations; happy to remain in the perceived security of own "cave."

6/3 Can be unforgiving or a little sarcastic with those who don't seem to appreciate his or her "counseling." Perfectionist tendencies could choke off creativity. Feelings of inadequacy cause anxiety because of doubts about ability to succeed. As a result, would rather be perceived as lazy rather than stupid and therefore doesn't try.

A variation of this pattern would be a tendency to overcommit. May scatter energies by trying to do too much for too many, with insufficient time or resources. May be a martyr.

Another pattern may be that of being ungrounded and therefore having no concept of personal responsibility. Alternatively, may refuse responsibility because it will force participation in life.

1	2	3	4	5	6	7	8	9
A	B	C	D	E	F	G	H	I
J	K	L	M	N	O	P	Q	R
S	T	U	V	W	X	Y	Z	

Table of Predefined 1st Vowel/1st Consonant Challenges   109

7/3 Can become disappointed, hurt, or resentful if wisdom and insights (even if unasked for) are not accepted as gospel, reinforcing underlying feelings of insecurity or inadequacy.

With this combination an individual may be more of an observer of life than a participant for fear of making a mistake or being embarrassed, humiliated, blamed for the failure of others, betrayed, abandoned, or misunderstood by others.

At an extreme, this individual may totally withdraw from life.

8/3 May try to dominate through a sharp tongue or bullying. If creativity is not appreciated, could become disloyal.

Feelings of inadequacy could hinder these individuals from becoming self-empowered.

9/3 Likes, almost needs, to do for others. Likes to be creative and dramatic in solving problems and then looks for recognition, appreciation, and thanks. If recognition is not forthcoming, can become unforgiving, moody, noncommunicative, or angry.

COMBINATIONS WITH NUMBER 4
Issues Involving Details and
"Getting Things Done"

Combinations with the number 4 involve issues of control and procrastination. A negative emphasis on 4 can result in a person who is prejudicial, reactionary, procrastinating, unimaginative, lost in minutiae, stubborn ("goes by the book"), confrontational, controlling, or overly logical (excluding intuition).

1/4 Low self-esteem can lead to stubbornness or procrastination. Can have a need to maintain control of situations due to a lack of confidence or low self-esteem.

2/4 Distrust in the reliability or the dependability of others can make it

1 2 3 4 5 6 7 8 9
A B C D E F G H I
J K L M N O P Q R
S T U V W X Y Z

hard for this person to cooperate. Can also have a hard time letting go of emotional or sentimental attachments.

3/4 May use sarcasm to keep others in line. A lack of focus can make it difficult to complete projects. Grandiose ideas may delay the implementation of plans. May only be concerned with the concept, not the details.

5/4 Does not like change except when in the role of change agent, in which case change can't come soon enough; may be involved with too many things simultaneously to pay attention to the details.

6/4 Likes to give advice but doesn't want to be bothered by the details of how to resolve things; not in it for the long haul.

May be a perfectionist and could also be a micromanager if in a position of authority.

7/4 Concern over changes results in being overly analytical, stubborn, and possibly reactionary. Doesn't want to be caught off guard, which could lead to embarrassment or humiliation, or being blamed for the failures of others.

Either relies totally on logic or unrealistically believes someone, or something, will finish the job.

8/4 Likes to orchestrate and delegate but doesn't necessarily want to be bothered by the details. Alternatively, when in positions of authority may need to micromanage everything. Could have major abandonment issues. In management positions, likes to do it "by the book," his or her own book.

9/4 Wants recognition for planning abilities and organizational skills; can be egocentric and stubborn. Has a tendency to poke nose into other people's business. Definite control issues and a need to be recognized for good deeds.

COMBINATIONS WITH NUMBER 5
Issues Involving Change and Movement

Combinations with the number 5 involve issues of flexibility, moderation, and change. As part of their personality patterns, these individuals may be either too rigid or too flexible (unbalanced), impulsive or reactionary, self-indulgent, inconsistent, promiscuous, or unable to control their appetites.

1/5 Fear of change and a lack of confidence can lead to rigidity (may be displayed as either aggressive or passive behavior patterns).

2/5 Needs the approval of others for changes or ignores the wishes of others and follows own inclinations.

3/5 Running in too many directions at one time, has difficulty finishing anything, or may seek to avoid participating in immediate setting due to insecurities, shyness, or anxiety.

4/5 Unless able to determine which changes will occur and when, will become overly cautious and a little stubborn when it comes to making changes.

6/5 Can be a perfectionist who has difficulty dealing with change or may be irresponsible, careening through life. May use the excuse that "everything is not perfect (or in place) and therefore no changes should be made." May also have a tendency to feel overly responsible for the welfare of others, which becomes an excuse for not moving forward in life.

7/5 Concern over being embarrassed, humiliated, or making a mistake causes hesitation or resistance to change.

8/5 Prefers to take charge, may have difficulty with alternatives suggested by perceived subordinates. As a leader may only deal in concepts, not details. May become easily frustrated with obstacles to success and either give up or dig in heels.

9/5 Likes to receive recognition of physical attributes. Ego may have difficulty dealing with the demands of the physical world. If stuck in a pattern of doing things to be loved or to maintain control, will use the excuse of "having to do for others" and not move forward.

COMBINATIONS WITH NUMBER 6
Issues Involving Family, Community, Relationships, Responsibility

Combinations with the number 6 involve issues of responsibility (accepting it or rejecting it), perfectionism, martyrdom, nosiness, being overly protective, difficulty making commitments, codependency, or avoiding obligations, commitments, relationships, or responsibility. Seeking validation of usefulness to others, may give unsought advice.

1/6 High expectations for self and others can make it stressful for both parties. May shy away from responsibility since accepting responsibility may result in being in the spotlight. Identity may be totally dependent on doing for or pleasing others.

2/6 Overly sensitive to the needs of others or can refuse to cooperate or accept responsibility. May be a bit of a micromanager, feeling responsible for the success of others.

3/6 Scatters energy by taking on too many responsibilities. Can be unforgiving of self or others because of high expectations or perfectionist tendencies.

4/6 Helpful but only on own terms. May have good intentions for self and others but rarely makes them a reality. Procrastinates because of a perceived sense of what perfection is but doesn't feel capable of achieving it. (As a child or immature adult, prefers to be called lazy rather than stupid and therefore seldom attempts anything new.) Also can be stubborn based on a false sense of "duty" or obligation to others.

1	2	3	4	5	6	7	8	9
A	B	C	D	E	F	G	H	I
J	K	L	M	N	O	P	Q	R
S	T	U	V	W	X	Y	Z	

Table of Predefined 1st Vowel/1st Consonant Challenges   113

5/6 May flee from responsibilities or put life on hold, using the excuse of having to do for others. May have a very rigid view of love, family, or service.

7/6 May feel a need to heal everyone, seeking to be validated for wisdom, compassion, and "goodness." (There can be major abandonment issues.) Fear of relationships comes from vulnerability issues. Social beliefs can be based on a self-righteous attitude (determining what is good or bad for others.) Can be interfering, demanding, overly analytical, bossy, anxious.

8/6 Wants to be the "authority" and tell others what to do but doesn't always want to be responsible for the outcome or may bully people into following his or her social beliefs.

In positions of leadership, may have unrealistic expectations of subordinates and what can be accomplished with the time and resources available.

9/6 Has a tendency to martyr self for love for either individuals or groups. Can either be insensitive or overly sensitive to the needs of others. There is a need to be needed and useful to the point of codependency.

Maintaining control of people or situations and having unrealistic expectations of self or others can create difficulty or friction in relationships with others.

COMBINATIONS WITH NUMBER 7
Issues Involving Abandonment, Trust, Skepticism, and Control

Issues revolving around abandonment are the catalysts for all negative 7 behavior patterns. Combinations with the number 7 involve issues of control, fearfulness, distrust, impatience, codependency, difficulty establishing and maintaining emotional connections, mental or emotional paralysis (associated with a tendency to overly analyze everything), zealousness, martyrdom, or messianic feelings. At the negative end of this spectrum of behaviors are individuals who think they can "beat" the system and may resort to devious or antisocial methods to do so.

1/7 With this combination, a person can be very withdrawn, aloof, self-absorbed, and fearful of being emotionally hurt. May seem aloof and disconnected to others. Can become fanatical when something involves cherished belief system. Such a person is what he or she believes, worthless or blessed.

2/7 Can be very impatient with others . . . "I see it, why can't/don't others?" May not speak up because of being either timid or overly sensitive to the feelings of others. Concerned about being "wrong" or misperceived by others and being humiliated, embarrassed, or ostracized as a result.

3/7 Can be moody and withdrawn, an intellectual bully, bitingly sarcastic, unforgiving, or demonstrate manic-depressive behaviors. A combination of impatience and scattered energy can lead to feelings of inadequacy, which can lead to self-flagellation.

4/7 Can be stubborn based on a fear of being wrong and thereby being humiliated and losing status in the community. May procrastinate due to concerns about potential for success or failure. Physical actions may be paralyzed due to being obsessively analytical to avoid failure.

5/7 May become physically rigid or paralyzed as a result of mental anxiety. Can be very impatient with the world, always needing to stay one step ahead of everyone else. On the other hand, may have a propensity for missionary work.

6/7 Intentions to help can be smothering or overwhelming to others. Fearful that others may make the wrong choices, is full of advice about what needs to be done and the best way to do it. Can be very controlling.

1	2	3	4	5	6	7	8	9
A	B	C	D	E	F	G	H	I
J	K	L	M	N	O	P	Q	R
S	T	U	V	W	X	Y	Z	

Table of Predefined 1st Vowel/1st Consonant Challenges   115

As a customer, will use a perceived flaw in the product as an excuse for not buying, rather than just saying no.

8/7 Has very firm opinions and no qualms about offering them to others. Can become anxious about things not in own control and therefore may try to dominate. May rely on facts and logic rather than intuition. May believe that "my way is the only way" and may throw a tantrum if can't have own way.

May be afraid (or not know how) to become self-empowered and thus allow self to be dominated.

9/7 Can act the role of a saint. Needs recognition and appreciation for good deeds. Can voluntarily become a pincushion for others' emotions. (Lower back problems can be associated with this behavior pattern.)

May be concerned about betrayal and therefore attempt to control the environment. May withdraw and refuse to be part of the world.

COMBINATIONS WITH NUMBER 8
Issues Involving Power, Money, Control, and Status

Combinations with the number 8 involve issues of frustration, money, self-empowerment, either a fear of success or a drive for success, bullying, control, and power.

1/8 Self-esteem is linked to the level of authority attained. Material acquisitions define success. As a defensive action, can be aggressive in establishing personal and professional boundaries.

2/8 May rely on others to manage or influence his or her personal and financial affairs. Hidden emotions can lead to difficulty with oral communications (e.g., stuttering, fear of speaking up, timidity).

Could be so forceful or controlling that relationships of any kind would be difficult; may have difficulty delegating tasks to others.

3/8 Can be sarcastic when enforcing authority. Can be emotionally volatile, up or down quickly. If managing multiple projects, attention can become so scattered that completion becomes difficult.

4/8 Logical to the point of stubbornness. Can be confrontational with authority or superiors. May be a reactionary, with the attitude, "If it ain't broke, don't fix it." Has a tendency to go "by the book" when in positions of authority.

5/8 Can be a rigid authority figure. Has the potential to squander finances or material holdings. Can be too impatient to be a leader. When in a position of leadership, may only pay attention to the concept and not the details.

6/8 May avoid financial responsibilities. May try to control group or family finances because of seeing self as the expert. High expectations for group members and an affinity for perfection can lead to stress for all. May want to be in charge but not want to accept the responsibility.

7/8 When in a position of authority, can have concerns over making mistakes or being embarrassed; may then become overly logical or analytical. Will always have "the final" answer or the last word. May be impatient with those who are not "in sync" with own ideas. May not trust intuition and instead rely strictly on logic.

9/8 Needs recognition and appreciation of leadership abilities. Could "blow a gasket" during emotional outbursts. Could be a benevolent dictator.

May opt out of the material world for the spiritual world; this is not based on altruistic motives but on either a fear of success or a feeling of not being "good" enough to be a success.

COMBINATIONS WITH NUMBER 9
Issues Involving Selflessness

Combinations with the number 9 involve issues of egocentricity, control, emotions, and codependency. From a negative standpoint, these individuals can be egotistical; need recognition/appreciation/thanks for their "good deeds"; have difficulty letting go of people, places, things, or emotions; be fearful of showing any emotion; be emotionally isolated or codependent; and hold the emotions and feelings of others like a reservoir holds water (especially in their lower back).

1/9 Can be emotionally intense. May be resistant about doing for others unless personal reward is implied. May demand attention from others but not be very giving in return.

Can lose self-identity in service to a group (whether secular or religious).

2/9 Can be either overly sensitive or totally insensitive to the needs of others. May seek love by joining groups, worry excessively, be codependent, or have a need to be in control, with difficulty letting go of emotional and sentimental attachments.

Will bend over backward to do for others until saturation point is reached; then just wants to be left alone and not disturbed.

3/9 Tries to do too much for too many with too little. May be moody (but moods pass quickly). An inability to socialize or communicate can lead to reclusive social behaviors. Needs to overcome feelings of insecurity and inadequacy and "be" in the world.

May scatter self in service to others because of feelings of inadequacy (unnoticed by others) and a wish for validation of usefulness. If a poor communicator, has feelings of inadequacy, may not be very sociable, could have difficulty with love.

May be a bit of a social climber.

```
1 2 3 4 5 6 7 8 9
A B C D E F G H I
J K L M N O P Q R
S T U V W X Y Z
```

118 Appendix I

4/9 Will do for others, but on own terms. May have good intentions about doing humanitarian work, but procrastination or getting lost in minutiae prevents completion. When trying to do "good deeds," can become idealistically rigid (his or her own logic is the only logic). Could have smoldering resentments over perceived mistreatment by others. Could be a curmudgeon (a killjoy or wet blanket).

5/9 May take risks based on emotional drives. Could have unpredictable emotional outbursts. Can be chameleon-like, hiding true feelings. May have major anxieties about life.

6/9 Can become a martyr by taking on responsibilities that others should be carrying. May be an impractical social reformer. Unrealistic expectations of/for others can make both parties unhappy.

7/9 May like playing god (Zeus is a 7/9 combination). May misuse knowledge for personal gain. May be resentful, have a "holier than thou" attitude, be noncommittal, or be overly analytical. Fear of abandonment or betrayal can make this person controlling.

A perceived lack of appreciation can lead to withdrawal from social interactions or just anger. Will remain aloof (emotionally and physically) until has time to "size things up" and decide how to proceed. May choose to be a recluse.

Because of a low sense of self-worth, might remain in an abusive relationship due to a fear of being alone, thinking no one will want him or her.

May become a religious zealot. Always doing for others first.

8/9 Relying heavily on logic, this individual finds people to be inconsistent in their behavior patterns and therefore desires to "direct" rather than participate. Financially, could be a "Scrooge McDuck" when it comes to spending money for social reform. Could have underlying frustrations and anger directed at the world in general, especially when things don't go as wished. Maintaining control at all times is important.

9/9 Highly emotional and very intense; could have a very short fuse. May have health issues initiated by intense emotions. Finds it very difficult to release attachments and move on.

Has a need to be loved; has difficulty letting go of or expressing emotions (may suffer from lower back pain as a result). May attempt to control environment and the people in it "for their own good."

APPENDIX II

Decoding Behavior Worksheets

The worksheets provided on the following pages will enable you to do an in-depth analysis, as they bring together in one place all of the primary Cosmic Numerology methods demonstrated in this book. Several copies are provided for your use. They include the compilation of the planes of expression results with achievement number, V/CC, and full name results.

As you work, keep the following in mind:

Your interpretations should be based on the birth name of the person (except in the case of adoption, when the adopted name should be used). However, if someone has legally changed his or her name, other than for marriage, use that name. In that case, you should use the day the court signed the papers as the person's birthday for the purpose of determining the new achievement number, as the choice of a new name is also a choice to be reborn, making the court date the person's new birthday. This brings in a complete new set of challenges. (However, if the old challenges have not been resolved, many of them will transfer to the new name.)

The person's complete name should be used to determine the numbers for the planes of expression.

Look for the repetition of the same number, as that indicates repetitive behavior patterns. (If there are two or more first or middle names, just use the V/CC for the first part of the name.)

When there are multiple first, middle, or last names, squeeze them together so they appear as a single, continuous name.

Worksheet Helpful Hints

- Instructions for deriving and interpreting the achievement number from the month and day of birth are given in chapter 2.
- Instructions for deriving and interpreting the V/CC of a name are given in chapter 4 (pages 41–50).
- Instructions for interpreting the combination of a name and an achievement number are given in chapter 4 (pages 53–59).
- Instructions for interpreting the first, middle and last name attributes are given in chapter 4 (pages 60–65).
- Instructions for deriving and interpreting the planes of expression are provided in chapter 5.

DECODING BEHAVIOR WORKSHEET

Achievement Numbers and V/CCs

Month and Day of Birth _____ = Achievement Number: _____

First Name _____ = V/CC _____

Middle Name _____ = V/CC _____

Last Name _____ = V/CC _____

Notes:

Name Attributes

Numeric Total of First Name Attributes _____

Notes:

```
1 2 3 4 5 6 7 8 9
A B C D E F G H I
J K L M N O P Q R
S T U V W X Y Z
```
Decoding Behavior Worksheets   123

Numeric Total of Middle Name Attributes _____

Notes:

Numeric Total of Last Name Attributes _____

Notes:

The Planes of Expression

First Name(s) _____

Middle Name(s) _____

Last Name(s) _____

	Mental	Physical	Emotional	Intuitive	Totals
Inspired	A	E	O R I Z	K	
Dual	H J N P	W	B S T X	F Q U Y	
Balanced	G L	D M	- - - -	C V	
Totals					

Dominant Expression: Mental   Physical   Emotional   Intuitive

Dominant Approach: Inspired   Dual   Balanced

DECODING BEHAVIOR WORKSHEET

Achievement Numbers and V/CCs

Month and Day of Birth _____ = Achievement Number: _____

First Name _____ = V/CC _____

Middle Name _____ = V/CC _____

Last Name _____ = V/CC _____

Notes:

Name Attributes

Numeric Total of First Name Attributes _____

Notes:

DECODING BEHAVIOR WORKSHEET

Achievement Numbers and V/CCs

Month and Day of Birth _____ = Achievement Number: _____

First Name _____ = V/CC _____

Middle Name _____ = V/CC _____

Last Name _____ = V/CC _____

Notes:

Name Attributes

Numeric Total of First Name Attributes _____

Notes:

Numeric Total of Middle Name Attributes _____

Notes:

Numeric Total of Last Name Attributes _____

Notes:

The Planes of Expression

First Name(s) _____

Middle Name(s) _____

Last Name(s) _____

	Mental	Physical	Emotional	Intuitive	Totals
Inspired	A	E	O R I Z	K	
Dual	H J N P	W	B S T X	F Q U Y	
Balanced	G L	D M	- - - -	C V	
Totals					

Dominant Expression: Mental   Physical   Emotional   Intuitive

Dominant Approach: Inspired   Dual   Balanced

DECODING BEHAVIOR WORKSHEET

Achievement Numbers and V/CCs

Month and Day of Birth _____ = Achievement Number: _____

First Name _____ = V/CC _____

Middle Name _____ = V/CC _____

Last Name _____ = V/CC _____

Notes:

Name Attributes

Numeric Total of First Name Attributes _____

Notes:

Numeric Total of Middle Name Attributes _____

Notes:

Numeric Total of Last Name Attributes _____

Notes:

The Planes of Expression

First Name(s) _____

Middle Name(s) _____

Last Name(s) _____

	Mental	Physical	Emotional	Intuitive	Totals
Inspired	A	E	O R I Z	K	
Dual	H J N P	W	B S T X	F Q U Y	
Balanced	G L	D M	- - - -	C V	
Totals					

Dominant Expression: Mental Physical Emotional Intuitive

Dominant Approach: Inspired Dual Balanced

Numerology Consultations with the Author

The creator of Cosmic Numerology, Michael Brill provides a variety of options for numerology readings and workshops, based on his mapping of the behavior patterns of the human personality matrix. He offers analysis of personal health and/or relationship issues, analysis and projections for businesses, recommendations on the best timing for various ventures, compatibility reports, and conflict resolution. For more information, visit his website or contact him by e-mail.

website: **www.awakener.com**
e-mail: **michael@awakener.com**

Index

```
1 2 3 4 5 6 7 8 9
A B C D E F G H I
J K L M N O P Q R
S T U V W X Y Z
```
Index   135

BOOKS OF RELATED INTEREST

Numerology for Healing
Your Personal Numbers as the Key to a Healthier Life
by Michael Brill

Numerology
With Tantra, Ayurveda, and Astrology
by Harish Johari

The Numerology of the I Ching
A Sourcebook of Symbols, Structures, and Traditional Wisdom
by Master Alfred Huang

A Study of Numbers
A Guide to the Constant Creation of the Universe
by R. A. Schwaller de Lubicz

The Prophet's Way
A Guide to Living in the Now
by Thom Hartmann

Shapeshifting
Techniques for Global and Personal Transformation
by John Perkins

2012: A Clarion Call
Your Soul's Purpose in Conscious Evolution
by Nicolya Christi

Healing the Mind through the Power of Story
The Promise of Narrative Psychiatry
by Lewis Mehl-Madrona, M.D., Ph.D.

INNER TRADITIONS • BEAR & COMPANY
P.O. Box 388
Rochester, VT 05767
1-800-246-8648
www.InnerTraditions.com

Or contact your local bookseller